UnCage Yourself

The Fearless Method to Turn Your Knowledge
into Market Influence, Impact and Income
to Live a Badass Life of Ultimate Freedom

HEATHER ANN HAVENWOOD

UnCage Yourself:

The Fearless Method to Turn Your Knowledge into Market Influence, Impact and Income to Live a Badass Life of Ultimate Freedom

Cataloged in publication information is available from Library and Archives U.S.

Paperback ISBN: 979-8-9877647-0-1

Hardback ISBN: 979-8-9877647-1-8

Contributors: Jonathan Grant and Stephanie Pierucci

Interior design by Jonathan Grant

Edited by Dale Chaplin

Cover design by Debi Quilla

ABOUT THE AUTHOR

Heather Ann Havenwood is an award-winning media mogul and top direct-response business marketer.

She is the author of the top selling books:

SEXY BOSS™

How Female Empowerment is Changing the Rulebook in Business Author

&

POWER GUESTING:

How to Get Leads and Grow Your Business Online with Podcasts.

Heather was recognized by The Stevie Awards™ (https://stevieawards.com/) as *The Most Innovative Woman of the Year – in Social Media for 2020*. She was also named *Top Media Mogul 2020* by the Woman of Achievement Association for her work with women.

From making her first dollar online back in 2001, Heather Ann is now on a life legacy mission: To help 1,000,000 people to Start, Launch and Grow a successful knowledge-based business online. She wholeheartedly believes that every person is an Influencer and a Leader— and that it is time for your VOICE to be UnCaged, to be heard, to shine and to earn Six-Figures and beyond!

Havenwood is the visionary and founder of the Influencer Growth Academy along with the Influencer Tribe, a global entrepreneurial community.

She is the podcast hostess of:

Heather Havenwood - UnCaged

www.uncaged.show

Insights with Influencers

She has also been named by Huffington Post as a Top Female Entrepreneur to Watch.

Further, she is the Founder of BossHub.ai.

Find more of Heather at:

HeatherHavenwood.com

I dedicate this book to my mentor Joe Sugarman, to Coach Kym, and to my mother, Julie: Thank you Mom for always loving me through it all. Rest In Peace.

FORWARD

by Frank McKinney

NEW YORK TIMES BESTSELLING AUTHOR OF:

Aspire: How to Create Your Own Reality and Alter Your DNA

I take risks. It's what I do. I'm a real-estate artist and speculative visionary who's sold 44 homes for an average price of $14 million. I'm a seven-time bestselling author. I'm an actor. I'm an ultramarathoner. I'm an aspirational speaker. I have purple hair.

I'm interested in the big picture and I like freedom—kinda like Heather Ann Havenwood.*

If you want to become the most liberated and most energized version of yourself, if you want to learn how to work less and make more, if you want to know the power and artform that is *influence and entrepreneurship*—then you should read this book and absorb what Heather Ann Havenwood has to say.

Her raw life-story lessons and UnCaged business methods will give you the mindset and tools that gift income and freedom. (It's ultimately up to you, of course, but they will help. Greatly.)

A 'Baptist girl gone bad,' Heather has overcome abuse, betrayal, bankruptcy, suburban hell, almost falling off a ski mountain, and one particularly terrible Covid-19 Bumble date to create three multi-million-dollar businesses and live life on her own terms.

She kicks ass. She takes names. She cashes checks.

And she'll show you how to do it too. She'll show you how to value your knowledge, how to leverage your knowledge, and how to sell your knowledge. She'll show you how to navigate the evolving marketplace. She'll show you how to navigate *people*. She'll show you when and how and why to make the deal. She'll show you how being weird is a good thing. And she'll make you smile while she does it.

See, beliefs do not determine behaviors—behaviors determine beliefs. And wherever you are at in the game, *UnCage Yourself* opens the doors that make you a believer in your own entrepreneurial and influencing potential. Right now.*

My first real-estate sale was a fifty-thousand-dollar fixer-upper. My most recent home sold for a Florida dollar-per-square-foot record amount. I did this by seeing things that others did not see—by being bold, by taking risks, by UnCaging from a world I did not believe in to soar in one that I did.

Kinda like Heather Ann Havenwood.

Kinda like you, once you read this book.

So, turn the page. In this book—and in your Life.

Rock On,

Frank McKinney

PREFACE

How's it goin'?! This is your author speaking. My name is Heather. Heather Ann Havenwood.

But I have to tell you: Havenwood is not my given name. I didn't like the old one so I changed it. Not by saying "I do," but because I wanted to. Because I like breaking free from cages.

And I like helping others break free from theirs too.

I'm an entrepreneurial consultant who's been named by *Huffington Post* as a 'Top 50 Must-Follow Women Entrepreneur.' I've won a Stevie Award™ for social media innovation, been crowned MS. TEXAS ELITE WOMAN OF ACHIEVEMENT, contributed to Entrepreneur.com and been called me "an eagle-eye authority on digital-marketing strategies and online business-sales systems."

I started my first online business in 1999 and have been playing an UnCaging role in the digital marketing world since before most homes had a computer.

In 2006, I started, developed, and grew an online publishing company from zilch to a million dollars in sales in less than a year.

Then I was duped. I lost it all. Duped by a male business partner.

So I started over.

I was pissed off and enraged, and I used it to sharpen my focus. I finally learned to protect my biggest asset: my knowledge.

In 2009, I started an online publishing newsletter business in the dating niche. I knew a lot about it, and I knew my knowledge could help other people. It did. That company soared, starting me back to rebuilding my empire. By 2015, I'd created a weight-loss and supplement business from zero to $1.5 million in sales in less than eighteen months.

I knew I could do it, and I wanted to do it, so I did it.

Just don't tell my uncle.

See, I grew up in a rigid, Southern Baptist, permission-based environment. A place where the women stayed home and took care of the house and the men went out and made the money.

"Heather," I remember my uncle telling me one day in my early 20s, "What are you doing with all this business stuff? I don't have to remind you, do I?"

"Remind me of what?" I asked.

"The truth—that *men* are entrepreneurs, not women. Stop living in a man's world."

I didn't listen to him.

(Neither should you when people try to keep you in your cage.)

Oh, and then there's my mom. She wanted three things for me. First, she wanted me to marry a rich and successful man. Second, she wanted me to be a good southern woman and have lots of babies. Third, she told me to never leave the house without looking amazing.

Well, mom, one out of three ain't bad. I like looking good, so I do. But I've never been married and I don't have kids. I wanted to be an entrepreneur. I wanted to have a nationally syndicated podcast. I wanted to write top-selling books. So, it is these things that I've done. And it is these things I will continue to do. And it is these things I will continue to help other people do.

Let's go! Your Time Is Now! You Are Ready To UnCage!

<u>UnCaged Lesson</u>:

Don't listen to advice that is not in alignment with YOURSELF. Pave your own path. Be your own creation.

TABLE OF CONTENTS

Understanding

Navigating

Core

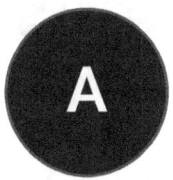

Audience

Genuine

Ease

Dominate

"Life is not about finding yourself.
Life is about *creating* yourself."

Heather Ann

U

Understanding

YOU ARE PAID FOR YOUR VALUE IN THE MARKETPLACE

The final door on Last Chance Road had just closed.

He was my dad for Christ's sake, and I didn't understand why he was doing what he was doing. I took my dog and piled what I could into my car. As I was about to drive away—to God knows where to do God knows what—my father opened his wallet and held out his hand. It was a ten-dollar bill. An Alexander Hamilton. Ten dollars. He gave me a high-and-mighty look and ten bucks. And then he spoke these words: "Heather, you are not welcome back here. You are no longer in my life. Do not come back."

I'd just lost it all in the 2008 recession—everything I'd built up by selling over $50 million from stages across the country. After leaving home at sixteen and building a multi-million-dollar business and having my own home and doing what I wanted to do, I was back down at the beginning again. I had half a tank of gas and a ten-dollar bill. I was hurt.

I couldn't believe I had turned to my family for help. I couldn't believe they pushed me out when I was down. My ego was battered. I looked out at the horizon and knew I only had two options: I could sell my body for money or make money using my mind.

At the fork in the road, I turned west. I would make it on my own. Again. I didn't know how I would do it. I just knew that I had to.

Though I didn't know it at the time, I had just been born into my second life, a life on my terms—a get-on-board-or-see-ye-later life that felt good.

I turned away from the road of expectations, the path of 'shoulds.' I turned west into the evening sun and kept driving until it arose again behind me.

I looked around again and found myself in Austin, where I put a six-hundred-dollar loan from a friend on an apartment. I didn't know what I would eat or how long the lights would stay on, but I had four walls, a roof, and a computer.

I got to work. But it was hard. A few days later I was sitting by the river under the Texas sun in tears, asking God, "What am I supposed to do? What's my path?"

And true enough I got a sign—from God or from my higher self or whatever. I just knew it was real. I could hear it clear as day, talking directly to me: "You are a creator, Heather," it said, "a powerful force of innovation. You are an Entrepreneur. Now, go! UnCage your mind and do what you do—create!"

Whatever that voice was; it changed my life. It really did. And for some reason, in that moment I had this vivid vision of an athlete—a world-class athlete, some bad ass playmaker like Serena Williams or something out there doing her thing. And it all made sense, how being an entrepreneur is really just a big game. It is the game of creating or extracting value from the marketplace. Like athletes, we try to win. Though the rules constantly change in our field, the way to win remains the same: boldness and innovation.

It does not matter what business you are creating. As long as you are creating value in the marketplace, you are an entrepreneur.

I instilled this.

In my moment with God by the river, I'd heard the voice. Now I just needed to create something, anything, that people would value. It could be rocket ships or it could be cupcakes. I thought to words spoken by Jim Rohn back in the '80s:

"You are paid for your value in the marketplace."

Those words from are more relevant today than ever. For what the market valued back then is not what it values today, and the market today is so much more faceted. Values and forms of expression change, constantly and all the time. That is why it is time to ditch old mindsets and seek new horizons. It is time to get rid of limits.

No more boundaries and never look back. Even though your boss may not value you, if you attack it boldly the market will.

Be bold. That's what a lot of my message is about. Because it works. For many others and for myself. Sure, it's been an up-and-down-and-up-again ride, but being bold has worked on my entrepreneurial journey.

And I know it can work for you too.

The truth is, there are a lot of people out there with 'the next great idea.' But only a few of them, I've learned, are ever bold enough to turn that idea into action.

UnCaged Lesson:

Your knowledge is valuable. Own it. Wield it. Be bold with it.

THE OLD GUARD IS DEAD

Y ou picked up this book so I'd wager that deep inside of you, you know that you have unique value. You know you can become an entrepreneurial force.

You are intelligent and you know it.

You see things that others don't.

Your mind gives you glimpses. Your life gives you glimpses. But you just haven't put it all into action. *Yet.*

That's okay. Right now, just know this:

Entrepreneurial knowledge has nothing to do with schooling. It has everything to do with understanding what the Marketplace desires.

Our schools and social constructs never really taught us how to sell our knowledge. I know mine didn't. They taught us how to get a degree and then go sell ourselves off at a one-time interview-auction; get our *one* job for a long and glorious career; wood-framed plaques of achievement, mid-size sedans, two weeks off a year.

Well, welcome to an UnCaged, Breaker-of-Chains, knowledge-based society with an overhauled rulebook that makes *everyone* a CEO if they are ready.

The old structure of a four-year degree plus a years-long climb up the payroll ladder is exactly that: old. Tired, dying, decaying, gone. The old guard is dead.

The word *boss* doesn't even play anymore. We are creators and collaborators; co-humans. The iron bars for gaining influence and impact in the market are widening. And for those ready to UnCage and rip them the fuck open, the world—and your place in it—is literally without limits. The great thing? It's really not all that hard. We've moved the world a bit on tilt. The little guy or girl—if he or she's got knowledge and hustle—has gotten into influence.

The big guys don't like it, because the playing field has been leveled. (Finally.)

The market is now a freelance, open-source, knowledge-based opportunity-zone ripe for any bold humans with unique knowledge.

So, I just have to ask you. Are you ready?

UnCaged Lesson:

Your time is now. You are ready.

BE AS BOLD AS THIS 'BOSS BABE' AND YOU GOT A GOOD SHOT

I learned about this historical entrepreneur once. She was born way back, born as Sara Breedlove only to change her name to C.J. Walker. I call her the original self-made woman.

C.J. was the daughter of former slaves in the sharecropping. She worked the fields. That's what her family did, and so that's what she did. She kept her head down and did what she was told. Life was hard. At age seven, it got harder when her parents died. She was an orphan with no plan.

She went on a few years living here and there, eking by. But she was always a devoted learner—books, pamphlets, two-week-old newspapers, the natural environment—anything and everything about how her world worked and why it was so.

C.J. accrued great personal knowledge, of herself and of her world. And she developed a growing sense that she could somehow add value to it. She learned and sought opportunity. Then, when a scalp ailment led to her hair to start falling out, she developed and sold a healing balm that actually proved to be pretty darn effective. She called it *Madam Walker's Wonderful Hair Grower*,

The stuff sold out.

C.J. couldn't keep up with the demand on her own, so she made the move to open a factory. She made more of her product and sold it out. Then she learned more and developed a full product line.

Within five years of the decision to become an entrepreneur—at worse odds than you or I will ever face—the Madame C.J. Walker Manufacturing Company had taken off, bringing in today's equivalent of multi-million dollar-a-year sales.

Then, in 1917, C.J. put on one of the very first organized meetings of businesswomen in the world. She spoke from the podium and energized the crowd with powerful words powerfully spoken. Sarah Breedlove had become Madam C.J. Walker. She'd done it. She'd UnCaged in a big damn way. And she shows us that we all can.

C.J.'s story reminds us of a few things about breaking free, about the mindset we must all have in order to do so. We've got to be smart, true, but we gotta be bold. The only limits are the limits we put upon *ourselves*.

Extraneous is nothing; C.J.'s parents were slaves for God's sake. But she fought. She was a rebel. And she created a product so good, so in the moment, that it didn't matter that she was a woman. It didn't matter that she was black. It didn't matter that she was poor. It didn't matter that she had callused hands.

She created something that made her and others in the world feel more beautiful. And she was paid for it. And she elevated her freedom because of it.

Just like we all can.

The rules weren't working for C.J., so she changed the rulebook that she played from. She emboldened, and she shocked the world.

It all reminds me of a quote:

> "BOLDNESS HAS GENIUS. POWER AND MAGIC IN IT."
>
> —JOHANN WOLFGANG VON GOETHE

You may have heard Goethe's words before, but have you ever truly tried putting them into practice? Have you ever truly *lived* that quote as C.J. did?

Without boldness, our true value will never be seen.

When I launched my book, *Sexy Boss™: How the Empowerment of Women is Changing the Rulebook for Money, Success, and Sex,* I was told that it was a fairly bold title.

Well, yeah. The whole thing was a bold move. People were coming up to me, specifically older men, with things like: "Heather, this whole *Sexy Boss™* book thing's not a good idea. Women don't want to be a 'boss,' they just want to be 'sexy.' What's all this about? Go find yourself a husband."

Yeah? Well, other people came up to me and told me how much the book had helped their life—women *and* men, young *and* old—how much it had transformed their life.

See, when you're bold, not everyone is going to like your idea or your knowledge; sometimes, not even *you.* Not everyone's going to stand in line to jump on board. That just isn't gonna happen. The road to success is littered with haters and doubters.

But if you never piss anyone off, you're not acting bold enough.

Susan B. Anthony? Pissed people off. Martin Luther King Jr.? Pissed people off. Daenerys Targaryen? Pissed people off. They shook things up and people loved them for it. That's what boldness does; it's like an intoxicant. True, some may run—but others will flock. To you.

Let me ask you a question.

Have you ever been told you're too much of something—too loud, too quiet, too big, too thin, too this, too that, too much, not enough?

Me too.

Well, I remember a guy on a podcast I listened to not long ago, and he shared a story about how he was not considered "black enough" to become a voice for the African American community.

He took a lot of flack for it.

But then the guy did something truly bold. He didn't use the critique as an obstacle but a springboard; he went on to make his mark *because* he 'wasn't enough' of something. That was his unique—and he owned it.

What I am trying to say is: if you are 'too much' or 'not enough' of something, then you're on the right track.

Henry Ford perfected the assembly line a long time ago; we've moved on. Today it's about being *different*: too much, not enough, too girly, too sexy, too manly, not manly enough… whatever. Rejoice in who you are and what you find interesting. Believe in yourself and others will too.

Get out of the main current so you can take a dip in the tributary waters of boldness. It won't wash off. Rock the flippin' boat, and if you get thrown overboard, swim. You'll find new shores.

When you are an UnCaged Entrepreneur, boldness is the propeller to your journey. It makes you 'go.' Any fence-sitting yes-girl can keep a job because she never pisses anyone off, but she's going to live and die in her cage because she lacks the courage to ruffle some feathers.

Say this out loud: *Boldness equals Success.*

Once more…

Boldness. Equals. Success.

Sure, being bold might make you 'fail' once or twice, but those aren't really failures. No, they are necessary steps along the Way.

I made my millions, like a lot of other people, by out-bolding the crowd. If you want to create value for the ever-evolving market and get paid what you deserve, know that bold work will be rewarded.

Trust me.

Actually, trust C.J.

UnCaged Lesson:

Boldness equals Success.

EMBRACE YOUR WEIRD

When I first got to Austin, I decided I wanted to be an actress. Well, I decided I wanted to *learn* acting. I was fascinated by it. I thought it could help me expand myself. So, I went to this acting school, and as I look back on it now, I had my blonde hair up all big, high heels, cute dress, and I looked great.

The acting coach, though, well she couldn't be less like me: mid-60s, no hair dye, a heavy smoker. We were completely different people.

She took one look at me and said, "You're not a good fit."

"Um, I haven't even said anything yet."

She shook her head. "You're a walking typecast."

I was more than a bit miffed. My acting career was over before it even started.

Then, a couple of months later, she gave me a call: "I may have found an opening," she said in her gruff, throaty voice. "Stop by the class next week."

A second chance! I showed up at the time and place I was supposed to show up. I was all excited. My hair looked great. She gave me a role; it was to play some hundred-pound-overweight failed singer-songwriter.

"This isn't me," I said, looking at the script. "I can't do this role."

She looked at me like a folktale ogre. "That's my point, 'Heather Big Boobs.' It's called 'acting.'"

That's when I knew my acting career was over. Because... well... I'm me. I'm good at being me, and I'm not much good at being anyone else.

"Well, shit," I said. "Maybe I'll try stand-up."

I'd always loved comedians. The bravado to get up on stage, just you and the mic, and try to make people laugh. It has to be one of the hardest things to do on the planet: people in the crowd just looking at you and saying, "make me laugh!"

But I've always liked a good challenge. After it only took about .234 seconds to learn that acting wasn't my cup of tea, I signed up to take a stand-up class.

It was fun. I liked it. I felt way more at home in it than in the acting class because it was all about being me and not someone else.

I made my classmates laugh, and the instructor at least didn't seem to hate me. Things were going well, but then I was told that to graduate we would actually have to do a 'five whole minutes' in front of a live audience.

What?!

So, I was working on my bit the day before the show, putting in the final touches—and I started to freak out. It was no good and I knew it. My act wasn't authentic to me.

So I looked up some other comedian coaches in the area and gave one a phone call. I explained my situation.

"Can you help me?" I asked.

"I can," he said with the confidence of Patrick Swayze. "My fee is fifty dollars. I'll see you on Skype in an hour."

I hung up. I got my hair looking good, put on a cute outfit and my cross necklace, and got ready for the video call that I hoped would save my first stand-up gig.

The meeting began. The guy took one look at me and gave a little nod and a chuckle. "So... you're the 'blonde, big-boobed, Baptist bitch.'"

"Huh?"

"Heather," he said, off-cuff, "the thing about comedy is to embrace exactly who we are, the things we like and the things we don't like about ourselves—and then double down on them. That's the authenticity the audience craves."

I again said, "huh?"

"Chris Farley was 'the crazy fat guy.' Amy Schumer, she made it by being the 'single slut in New York.'"

My "huhs" turned into an "ohhh...," and I was beginning to understand.

"So, yeah," he continued, "you're the big-hair, big-boobed, Baptist-girl-gone-bad bitch. Own it."

He was telling me *not* to take the advice I'd been getting my whole life, the advice that said, "Don't be so loud." The advice that said, "Cut your hair!" The advice that said, "Don't be Sexy. Shrink your boobs."

"Just own it?" I asked.

"Just own it," he said.

I did. We worked on my schtick. He got me to double down on the parts of me that had always been thought of as "over the top;" the things that made me, *me*; the things that I could use to make an audience laugh.

That last-minute comedian coach got me to *embrace my weird*.

I gave him my fifty bucks and a virtual hug, and the next day I gave my five minutes on stage as a stand-up comedian in front of a live audience. After a no-energy opener (the instructor of the class, mind you (I felt sorry for him)), I walked in from the back of the room whooping and hollering and raising the roof by being loud and silly.

I walked up on stage, grabbed the mic like a boss, and said, "My name's Heather—and I'm a big hair, big-boobed, Baptist-girl-gone-bad bitch!"

The audience chuckled and hollered out.

I was in.

And for the next five minutes, that little theatre was filled with big laughs. Laughs made by me celebrating me, by doubling down on me.

It was a big UnCaging moment in my life.

The lesson? In business (and life), don't act.

No, be you.

Double down on you.

Double down on the parts of you that were made fun of when you were a kid.

Because these are the parts of you as an adult that make you intriguing.

UnCaged Lesson:

Double down on your weird—you'll get more respect, have more fun, and make a lot more money this way.

UNDERSTANDING YOUR INNATE VALUE.

L et's get real. The new value in the marketplace is influence. The new value lay in the ability to move people into action through emotion. That is influence, and that is what people are looking for.

So, for this new value, what is the new currency?

I call it "relationship currency." It defines what you give, humanly, for what you will get, economically. It is people-to-people power. And if you can do it, you will get paid.

To have a high relationship currency, you must first 'understand your why.' You must understand, and know in-depth, your entrepreneurial purpose. Money can't be your sole purpose. It's got to be bigger than that. It's got to have soul. You've got to ask yourself, "What is the impact I am bringing to other people's lives?"

To answer this question, you have to understand the currency of value. A lot of entrepreneurs who are still getting their feet wet look at 'hours of work' as currency.

Well, that's old thinking. That's old currency. As an entrepreneur, you're not 'clocking in' anymore. You're *creating*—it doesn't have to take that long. An idea may strike you in a second—and in that one single second, you can create value that forty years of punching the timecard could not.

It used to be all about the loyalty to the company: "Valerie has worked here for forty years and never taken a sick day," type stuff.

Yeah, well Valerie should have taken some days for herself because the company made a hell of a lot more money on her than she made from them.

The new loyalty is to yourself. It's not like old Hollywood anymore; we aren't told who the new star is going to be. In the new market it's not just Tom Cruise or Jennifer Aniston who get to be the star. We all can be the hero—if we learn what we need and if we want it bad enough.

It is a great time to be an influencer entrepreneur.

But with this new and tremendous opportunity comes competition. One of the best ways to rise above the rest, to truly understand your innate value and bring it to the forefront, is to make your life 'one big room.'

In the old paradigm, we had a work life and we had a home life; we had a family life and we had a social life. It was all compartmentalized. But the UnCaged way of thinking is to break down all those walls.

In the early 2020s, for example, the companies that took a stand on social justice saw a forty percent increase in their value across the board. The companies that decompartmentalized their business room and their social awareness room and joined them in one big room, grew.

Conversely, companies that kept those rooms compartmentalized, who didn't incorporate a stand for some kind of social justice, remained where they were or took a dive.

The market valued the 'one big room' approach.

Therefore, as an entrepreneur what you stand for (or against) goes a long way to defining what you are and how the market sees you. You are not simply selling some new widget or a revolutionary consulting strategy; you're selling a comprehensive vision of who you are. And, really, *this* is your innate value.

Serve others and make your entrepreneurial life one big room—business, friendship, passion, fun, wealth, and influence all existing together. Connect all that you do and all that you are, and great things can and will happen. Watch how *exponential* the results are in your business, in your community, and in your life once you stop trying to control the separation and instead focus on your connectivity.

Take it from me. I'm a controller by nature. I've had to work hard to learn how to allow—how to <u>accept</u>. I encourage you to not take as long as I did.

Allowing and finding flow is a real thing. The need to feel control over everything is a dam. The need to exert control over everything stops the growth of everything. Don't let it.

Expand your people-to-people relationship currency, make your life 'one big room,' and allow your maximum innate value to bloom.

<u>UnCaged Lesson</u>:

When we relax our grip, we allow things to come. It is then that we scale our impact and increase our income.

Navigating

AN EARLY CAGE

I grew up in the upper-middle-class Texas suburbs where everything and everyone were literally the same. Dressed the same. Acted the same.

I swear, everyone *thought* the same.

All my friends and 'mentors' from early life were like, this is a girl's life plan: prom queen, four-year degree, husband, kids; build up a high tolerance to gin, hide your muffin-top and varicose veins, and then spend the golden years looking back at it all in some sepia-toned lens of satisfaction; death, and a fabulous funeral where everyone talks about what a great human you were.

Well, something like that. And I bought into it. I flung the pom-poms, chased the boys, and got good marks. I did the dance and I got into Baylor Baptist University, like a good little Baptist Girl would, right? Then that myth of what I "should do" all came crashing down.

One morning during my first semester, I was in this all-girls bible study class. As we were introducing ourselves—sharing where we were from and the degree we were pursuing—four out of four of the girls said, with all the seriousness of a heart attack, that the degree they were pursuing was their "M.R.S. Degrees."

"M.R.S?" I said, curious. "Is that like a Master's... in Respiratory... Science?"

Laughter erupted throughout the room. And they weren't laughing *with* me.

"Oh, honey," some girl said. "Aren't you sweet? M.R.S. degree, like 'Misses.' You know, Mrs."

"Heather," another one said. "I'm here to find me a husband. Plain and simple."

I leaned back in my chair. I'd just learned a big lesson. A big lesson that the world I was living in was too small for what I wanted to achieve in my life—and that I needed to break free from it. That breaking free from this cage and all the others I would encounter on my journey was imperative for my survival.

So, dear UnCaged-bad-ass-entrepreneur-reader—what are you going to break free from today?

What are you going to break free from tomorrow?

The next day?

What tired paradigms are you going to continue to break free of so you can achieve ultimate freedom?

> ## UnCaged Lesson:
>
> Choose who you are choosing to be.

SUGARMAN STORIES

Joe Sugarman was a legend. Among about a million other things, he created the Batman Credit Card and those BluBlocker® Sunglass infomercials from the 80s.

The dude was the direct response copywriter king. Joe could sell sand to the beach. With his words, he could make people pick up the phone and buy. Anything.

He's now passed, but he was been a big mentor of mine for decades (even wrote the forward to my previous book, *Sexy Boss*™), and I learned a ton about business from him.

We did a conference together, the Success-Magnet Seminar, in Las Vegas. A bunch of the top copywriters were there—Joe Polish, Jon Benson, John Carlton. It was a great conference where a lot of good teaching and learning took place.

I'd already heard Joe speak dozens of times and was looking forward to another one. He was a truly gifted speaker. And one thing I'll say about Joe: he was not afraid to tell the same stories over and over and over again. Huge conferences, with a high percentage of people who'd heard Joe speak previously, and Joe was up on the stage with the same punchlines, the same stories, and the same lessons.

"Ever think about mixing up the stories?" I asked him one day.

"Why?" he said, a touch of surprise in his voice.

"Because people have heard them before."

"They're coming back, aren't they?"

And it hit me. The obviousness of the truth. Of course they were. People loved the stories he told, the lessons they taught; perhaps, even in some genius way of Joe, they loved the predictability of them.

After his address the next day, this guy came up to Joe and literally said, "I saw you four years ago Mr. Sugarman, and you told the same story. I loved hearing it again."

Yep.

Because Joe knew if it wasn't broke don't fix it. If something is getting the desired results, keep going with it. Hone the heck out of it. Sharpen it. Perfect it.

And don't recreate something if you don't have to.

In 'n' Out Burger out on the West Coast is great this way. Since 1948, its menu has remained unchanged. Hamburger, cheeseburger, double-double, fries, shakes, soda. Never a chicken sandwich, chicken nuggets, or a salad. Because, like Joe and his stories, they identified that they had something that worked and they stayed with it.

Most of us entrepreneurs will do more storytelling than hawking burgers, so remember this: it's okay to tell the same stories over and over. It's counterintuitive, but it works.

We watch our favorite movies over and over, don't we? Even though we know how it ends, we watch it because it's *that* good. I know I watch *The Christmas Story* every Christmas. Ever heard a song more than once? Course you have.

Joe would tell me how storytelling is not so much a gift but a *learned* skill. And he would tell me how it is key, *the* key to everything—how the stories you tell about your product, the stories you tell about what you do and how you do it, are central to the value you will add to the marketplace.

Bill Gates created a story around what he was doing. Jeff Bezos created a story for Amazon. When we were kids, telling a good story to our parents would allow us to go to the movies versus doing homework on a school night: "But Mom, I really need to go because. . ." And you thought of what story would make her let you go.

Stories. Practice them. Get two or three really good ones and tell them over and over. And make sure they have a lesson in them, a moral to the story.

And then find avenues upon which to use them.

In 2015, I launched my own podcast show and started focusing on being a guest on other people's podcasts. To date, I have been on over 450 podcasts and other media appearances, just as a guest alone. The fact that I launched my own podcast has made me an attractive guest for others. It's great. I get to speak, to share my message without having to do much but have a conversation with someone on their show. I share many of the same stories over and over again. I found that, for instance, no matter the subject of the podcast, my story of going from "millionaire to broke to Sexy Boss author" played well because it was a universal human story. It connected to people and allowed me to share my message—how we can all rise out of the ashes to UnCage and do big things

I have fun with my guest appearances. You can too. Virtual speaking is fun, and being a guest on someone else's podcast can help take the pressure off. You're not the one pushing play, you just get to go in and do your thing and keep building your audience. You get to grow your list and continue to increase your visibility and authority.

And you can do it with three stories that you tell over and over again. That's why in my mentorship program I help creators craft their "3 Signature Stories." We get them honed. We get them adaptable and ready to fling off the cuff—on virtual events, podcasts, stages, and more.

So, to you, bad-ass UnCaging Entrepreneur, I encourage you to get your "3 Signature Stories" crafted. Dig into the memory bank. Find three things you've experienced that are human and universal. And hone the telling of them.

UnCaged Lesson:

To gain influence, embrace the storyteller inside of you.

THINK BIG

I always wanted to go to law school, but my father hated lawyers. Despite his negativity, at 22 years old I was more excited than ever about going to law school. It was Thanksgiving Day. I'm at my father's house with my half-brother and half-sister. I go into the TV room, and I tell my half-brother, "Hey, I'm going to tell Dad that I want to go to law school."

His eyes grew big and wide. He whisper-yelled, "Don't tell dad that, he'll freaking flip out!"

Well, of course, I go right up to dad after dinner and tell him. Because, I'll admit it, a lot of what I wanted was his permission. I wanted my father to be like, "Of course. If that's what you want, honey."

Nope.

You know what my father did? He sat me down in the living room for the next three hours and told me why, exactly, emphatically, my going to law school was a stupid idea from a dumb little girl.

I just wanted him to be proud of me. I wanted him to approve of me. I wanted his permission to go to law school.

He didn't give it.

I was young.

It sucked.

And I didn't go to law school because I wasn't strong enough to permit myself to do so on my own. I sought permission and validation outside of myself. My father wasn't there to give it to me, and I wasn't strong enough to do it on my own.

Now when I have a mission—something I must do—I just go and do it. I often don't even tell people what I'm going to do until it is done. I no longer need their permission.

Many of my author friends will entirely cease reading other books until they complete their manuscripts. They do this because they don't want outside influence on their style or their work. They are protecting their energy.

They know what they need to do, and they just do it.

These authors are a great example to follow because it's the same with entrepreneurship.

And, what's an entrepreneur again?

Yeah, someone who creates. Someone who creates VALUE in the marketplace—creating something that wasn't there before and bringing it to the market with boldness and clarity.

So, go after your desires, dreams, and big ideas. Do it. Be and create and sell. Dream and do and fly.

Don't let anyone else hold you back. Go for it. You have the power to turn that dream into your reality.

From second grade on, we are taught to raise our hand for permission to even go to the bathroom. When I was eight, I once waited for permission "to go" for so long that I peed in my pants.

But to be an UnCaged Entrepreneur, we must escape the permission-based mind frame and just go and fricking create!

It's a good place to start, anyway. And the rest has a way of falling into place.

Recently, I was vetting this client, testing her out to see if I would take her on, and so I asked her what she really wanted; how *big* it was.

She breathed deep and said, timidly, "You know what, I haven't really told anyone because—because it's pretty big. And I'm afraid people will think I'm crazy."

"Great!" I told her. "If it's a crazy idea, it's got legs."

UnCaged Lesson:

The bigger and crazier the idea—the better.

THINK DIFFERENT

In his book, *Mastery*, Robert Green details stories from some of history's most influential people: Julius Caesar, Catherine the Great, Albert Einstein, and a bunch of others. It's a great book, and it gives an insight into what all masters have; their differences, and their core similarities.

I want to touch on Einstein real-quick. He was a fairly smart guy, the theory of relativity and all that?

Yeah, and he did a heck of a lot more too. In numerous fields. He was always on the cutting edge. When he got somewhere, he was already thinking about where he could go next. Always the next thing. Further. Higher. Deeper.

So much so, that it was too much for a lot of his contemporaries.

When he got his first degree, Einstein was just another young man who needed a job. So, he went back to the university and applied for a job as a researcher. I mean, who wouldn't want to have a young Albert Einstein on the team, right?

Well, apparently, not his alma mater. Nope, he was denied that entry-level researcher position.

"Too cutting edge," they probably said. "Too smart. Too *weird*. Not a good fit."

Sound familiar?

UnCager, there may come a time (or perhaps you've already experienced it) when you will be told that you're not a good fit. That your vision doesn't match that of the business. That you're too out of the box. That you don't color within the lines.

Great.

It means that you *think differently* than other people, that you see things your own way.

And it is when we see things our own way that genius happens. When one door closes, a larger door often opens.

Ol' Albert is on record saying, "I have no special talents. I am only passionately curious."

Well, if he would have toned down that curiosity to mold to the expectations of that university researcher job, he would have been unfulfilled—and the world wouldn't be what it is today.

> ## UnCaged Lesson:
>
> Albert Einstein wasn't willing to cage himself for some job-job.
> You shouldn't either.

NAVIGATING THE SEAS
OF COMMERCE

It may look like our society is conformist, but the reality is that people are looking for leaders, looking for influencers, looking for people that break the mold. People and money follow leaders that are aspired to. People and money follow influencers who are exciting to follow. With Millennials and Generation Z, this looks a lot different than it did for Gen X and the Baby Boomers.

Polls show that consumers under the age of 40 don't trust companies and largely hate politics. They see these entities as "pay to play," and they don't jive with it. They see themselves as outside this archaic thinking.

The younger consumers see themselves as a force recreating the world. And, in a very tangible sense, they *are* doing this—in a few ways, not the least of which in how and what they buy.

They've changed the market, changed what it values from "what is consumed" to "what is *followed*." Millennials and GenZ buy from brands and companies who they feel understand them. Plain and simple. This market-shift reflects that the younger generations are getting what they want. The market isn't top-down anymore. It's built from the bottom up, from the people... how it should be.

The way big companies used to advertise—in the yellow pages, on billboards, and on pages of magazines and websites—was by selling "direct to the consumer."

That's old thinking.

The UnCaged world is all about selling *through* the consumer. A whole new tactic. A big change. Not "to the consumer" but "through the influencer."

Yet, while this change has been driven by younger generations, *everyone* wants to feel that when they buy something, it was recommended by someone they trust.

This person, today, is not some celebrity on a TV commercial who everyone knows is just doing it for a paycheck. In today's influence market, it is a trusted human being (could be a celebrity but it no longer has to be) vouching for the product or service.

People want an influencer to influence them.

And the market has seen this, which is why Influence Marketing is what it is today.

In my mentoring program, Influencer Growth Academy, I mentor influencers through a year-long program that immerses them in business mastery. We go from Sponsorship 101 all the way through to their speaking and book tours.

Today's consumer doesn't necessarily need to feel like they trust the company; simply the personal brand. Even Warren Buffet recently said that in today's marketplace, establishing your personal brand is one of the biggest moves you can make to increase your personal net worth.

Today's market reflects a much more personal approach to buying and selling, and that personal approach is the international language of influence. It is a language spoken across generations and cultures, through language barriers and time zones.

And to help you gain fluency, you must understand that the new economics is social currency.

I can't say that enough—*the new economics is social currency.*

The new economics is the value that people put on you because of what you know and how you can persuade others to know it.

And a lot of people in business today are "solo entrepreneurs." Gig workers, 1099 employees. People that work for themselves.

This trend is not some fad. It was here before the pandemic, and it is only growing. The empowerment of the solo entrepreneur is here to stay.

We all have a laptop and a cell phone—that is a bat and a glove to take to the field of business and play some ball.

And, odd as it may seem, the more out of the box you appear, the higher your social currency becomes. It's all the stuff from the last chapter about "embracing your weird."

The funkier you are, the more *unique* you are. And in a world of solo entrepreneurs, the figurative "loudest dress" or "most outrageous boa" gets wooed the hardest.

But Heather, you ask, why?

To be blunt, it's because we are all weird. Every last one of us human beings. And, collectively, we are tired of hiding it. The old way was trying to tell us that we are all the same. The old way was striving for us "to be normal." That didn't work. It didn't work because there are eight billion of us and we all see the world differently.

Normal, now, equals death.

Crazy zany polka-dot leopard-print rocket-ship boldness equals commerce.

Which equals influence. Which equals your life, elevated.

We'll go deeper on this later. For now, it's enough for me to say, "Be solid in exactly who you are. It'll help you navigate the modern seas of commerce."

Take the leap. Even if you're a stay-at-home cat person: double down on being the most stay-at-homey cat person the world has ever seen. Own it. Create a brand from it. Your Personal Brand. Your Influencer Brand. Your UnCaged Brand. People will want to buy what you own.

UnCaged Lesson:

Your brand ain't no hobby. It's your life.

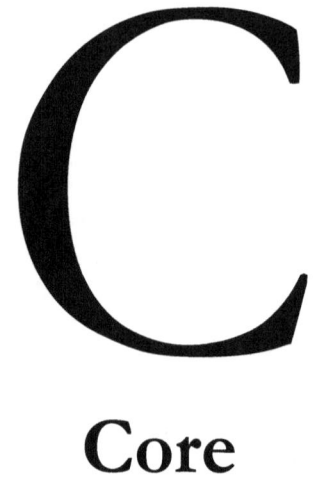

Core

NAKED AND UNCAGED IN A GLASS HOUSE NEAR YOU

To reach as many people as I can, I go LIVE on social media a lot. I like to, and I know I am good at it. So going live is one way that I know I add value to the marketplace.

And let me say this: When you go LIVE, yes, you *are* vulnerable. "Putting it all out there" for the world to see can be terrifying—all those people making comments, comments that can be so dang mean.

(Especially on social media. They don't have to look us in the eye or anything and they can *still* tell us we're no good.)

But here's what I know: with showing vulnerability comes a superpower: Showing vulnerability is the most authentic thing a human being can do. People respond to it.

Sure, it can take brass ovaries to make a LIVE. But if you're going to walk the UnCaged path, a good live video or audio goes a long way. This is because sometimes for us to succeed as an entrepreneur, we have to 'walk the plank.'

For a lot of us, that plank is going LIVE—in person or online. For we know that people can throw stones.

I heard it when I was young: "If you're living in a glass house, don't throw stones." Well, apparently, some people didn't get the memo. People will talk shit. People will hate. And, yeah, that stuff hurts. But odds are that if everything you do is received without question, you're probably playing it safe.

And no one will ever truly consume you if you are playing it safe. Hard as it is, we must put ourselves out there.

We remember the bad stuff, the hard stuff, the stuff that *hits*. But without it, we wouldn't know how far we can go. Kites fly highest against the wind.

So, get in front of audiences, go LIVE, and really put yourself out there. You got this.

Prepare.

Take your time.

Breathe.

Then give your solo by doing a LIVE, and become an entrepreneurial Breaker-of-Chains.

Be super bold.

And practice a golden rule of entrepreneurism: Be very careful at whom you jab. Stuff comes back. I've had to learn this the hard way a few times. Entrepreneurship can be a glass house. Along my entrepreneurial journey I've seen some shattered houses.

I knew this guy once who threw a stone from his glass house. He'd just moved his business over from live seminars to online events in response to Covid. He was working long hours to gain some steam. Things were slow, and then one day they finally clicked and his business was flourishing again.

But then, he threw a jab he shouldn't have.

He insulted a reputable online female marketer, a person who'd been crushing it at online marketing for years.

People knew her. They didn't necessarily know him, not in his new house.

And he threw a stone. He, in essence, posted something to the effect of *she doesn't know what the fuck she is doing, and I'm your guy.*

It shattered his glass house. Right then and there. With one comment, the dude lost all traction.

It cost him a business and his reputation. Cost him time and money.

If you're going to be successful, you're going to have to be willing to pick and choose your battles. Positively.

If you let *them* get to you, you're going to get negative. You may still make money, true, but you can do that by working for someone else.

The UnCaged entrepreneur doesn't have time to throw stones; she's too busy doing the work she knows she needs to do.

She doesn't have energy to burn bridges; because she's too deep into creating something new or perfecting something that's not yet perfect—because she knows those are the only two jobs we entrepreneurs really have.

To summarize:

Only throw a stone if you know the crashing glass will somehow help. (It usually won't.)

Walk into the room with confidence in your message and in who you are as a person. Put yourself on a stage. Show up and allow yourself to show off.

A lot of people won't notice, and some may somehow think you're the devil. But others will respond in positive ways beyond what you'd ever imagined.

> ### UnCaged Lesson:
>
> Be Confident in Your Message. Don't worry about the haters.

HELP WANTED! IN HOPE

It's 2002, and I'm living in Florida. Sort of. I travel for work. A lot. I'm living out of a suitcase for fifty weeks a year, traveling with top real estate investor-speakers and gurus from and around the country. I'm doing seminar after seminar every single week—seven to eight seminars per week, in cities all over—teaching people how to buy and sell houses, flipping real estate.

One day, I was at a conference with all these great real estate minds, guys like Robert Allen and Ron LeGrand. Tony Robbins was even there. I was like, "Tony and his great jawline just hanging out?!"

It was so amazing. I looked around, and had this thought that I'm *living this great life,* just surrounded by millionaires and thought leaders.

I leave the conference and I'm walking on air. I get to my car when the phone rings. I look at the number. It's my uncle. Not an uncle that would ever just call me.

I'm thinking someone's dead or someone's about to die—someone's in the hospital. I answer the phone: "My God," I say, fearful. "Why are you calling me?"

"Your mom called."

"Is she okay? What's going on?"

"She's fine. She's just concerned about you."

I'm listening to his voice thinking to myself, what? I'm a healthy 20-something with a sexy car who's hawkin' houses, speaking on stages around the country and banking money. I'm having fun. How in the hell is my mom concerned about *me?*

"She told me that you are starting a business," he explained.

"Well, yeah. I actually have a couple businesses."

"Heather," he says, "stop doing that stuff. You're freaking out your mother. You and I both know women aren't business owners."

I was stunned silent.

My uncle kept on speaking. "Stop being an entrepreneur, Heather. You are worrying your mother."

I just shook my head, hung up the phone and called my mom.

"Hel-lo," she says in her southern Texas drawl.

"Mom, it's me. I just got off the phone with Un—"

"Oh, honey! I'm so glad you called. I was talking with some friends recently—and I found you a job. It's perfect. It's a secretary position at a manufacturing plant over in Hope."

"Hope?" I said, confused.

"Hope, Arkansas. Good company. Pays a solid eight dollars an hour, and it's a lovely little town."

I shake my head again. Here I am living in Orlando making boats of money and having the time of my life—and my own mother is telling me to "stop doing all that nonsense," and to instead go and live in a Podunk town as an eight dollar an hour secretary?

WTF?

Somehow, though, I wasn't even mad at her. I wasn't mad at her because I knew that from her point of view, the path I had set upon as my own was "unsafe."

That was my mom's cage.

I, on the other hand, was breaking out of mine.

COMMIT TO THE MOUNTAIN

I love downhill skiing. I'm no pro, but I love it. I love being on the top of the snow and looking around, understanding how it's just me and the mountain. The silence of it, the freedom of it.

When I was young, I'd fall on my butt and be all embarrassed that someone may have seen me. But in time I came to learn something beautiful about skiing—no one cared.

Every other skier out there was just doing their thing. So I just needed to do my thing—just me and the mountain.

It's the same with entrepreneurship. There will always be a ton of other people doing their things in and around the market, making their left turns and their right turns, but all that really matters is what you are doing. In both skiing and entrepreneurship you must have a plan of 'where am I going,' and then focus on the present moment so you can follow through and adapt if need be. If there's a patch of ice in front of you, no one else is going to make that turn for you.

Skiing, I find, is a lot like being your own boss. Yeah, you can hire a ski instructor or a business mentor; you can watch YouTube videos on how to make a proper powder turn or read up on the latest trends in the market. But when it comes time to make a turn, to adapt and adjust and let it rip, it's got to come from within.

One February day a few years ago I was out in Lake Tahoe to ski with my mountain-man boyfriend of the time. It was beautiful—the mountains, the snow, the lake and the sky, David and his scruffy red beard.

I was at the top of Squaw Valley (Palisades Tahoe), and I'm way up there at the top, thousands of feet of steeps below me and the lake to the southeast.

I'm feeling good, but then I look down and realize, "Damn, this is *really* steep."

"Oh don't worry about it," David tells me. "We're going to traverse out a ways and then drop down when it looks good."

I think I trust this guy, but all of a sudden I'm not too sure. I look down the mountain. "Okay," I manage.

We start traversing out the ridge, following a skinny little ski track and the pitch seems to just fall off straight down to my right. We keep going, out way past where I thought we were going to go. David is out front and we're passing all these signs that say things like DANGER and DON'T GO THIS WAY and SKI AREA BOUNDARY.

I'm following this expert skier dude way out of my comfort zone, and my heartbeat is racing. "Weren't we supposed to drop in already?" I ask.

"Nah," David says like James Bond, "we're going '*off-piste*.'"

"Off *what?*"

Turns out 'piste' is some French word for going off the grid of the resort, out to where the runs aren't groomed and nature is in control. Unmarked obstacles, trees, cliffs, chasms, avalanches.

Whatever. He's my boyfriend and I think I trust him, so let's do this.

But then we keep going out further. Finally David drops into the steeps and skis on down, the powder blowing over his head as he makes his turns.

But I'd never skied snow this steep and deep. I started to get anxious. Thoughts of wanting to turn back surfaced. I took a breath. I looked around. And there was this moment of realizing that 'I could not turn around.' I knew I'd passed the point of no return, that there was no going back.

The only way was down.

I dropped in.

I literally sank two feet into the snow on my first turn, somehow keeping my momentum down the fall line and skiing a few turns down to David. He told me I was doing good. I didn't believe him. Then he hooted a hoot and took off charging down the slope, leaving me stranded far above him.

I turn to ski down and follow him. It is slow and difficult at first in the deep snow, but I'm getting the hang of it. I start to get this amazing feeling of weightlessness, this feeling of freedom. All was great.

Until it wasn't.

I fall.

I crash.

I yard sale deep into the deep snow. My left ski ejects and I tumble head over feet a few times. When I finally come to rest, my head is below my feet, and I can't move.

I look up, on the mountain, half buried, can't move.

From far down the mountain, I hear David's voice. "Try to unclick your other ski!" he yells.

"I can't move!"

But I had to. I knew David was too far down to help me. I could complain and cry, I thought, but then I'd probably just still be here when the sun went down and I'd freeze to death. If I was going to get out of this thing, I knew it was on me. But half buried in the snow, it was almost like the more I struggled the worse it got.

I took a breath. "One thing at a time," I told myself.

I calmed myself. I calmed my mind. I became present. I broke it down into second-by-second actions of what I needed to do. The next minute. The next breath. Now. What can I do to better my situation, at this moment, for the next moment?

In all this deep, heavy snow, how do I get my feet below my head, unclick from my buried right ski, find my ejected left ski, not kill my boyfriend, and get off the mountain before I freeze? How do I *survive*?

Yelling at David wasn't going to save me. Crying to myself wasn't going to save me. Getting present and conquering the moment was what was going to save me.

I had to commit to the mountain.

So I did.

Because I had to.

Commitment over convenience.

About an hour later I was unthawing in the village by the fireplace at Le Chamois drinking a glass of red and laughing about my "off-piste adventure" with David and a bunch of longhaired locals I'd just met. It was awesome.

I felt great. I was proud of what I did when I knew I had to do it. Buried in the snow, off the grid, David way too far below to help.

No ski patrollers to call. Just me and the mountain, and "how am I going to figure this one out?"

Just like you and the market—and how are you going to figure this one out?

UnCaged Lesson:

Become Your Own Hero.

CHOICES AND PRIORITIES

I knew early on in my life that my destiny wasn't going to be found living in the town where I grew up for the rest of my life. I knew I had to get out into the world and find myself. So what if I didn't have a tan line on my ring finger?

But after a few years I started getting a lot of flak from a lot of people in my life for not being settled. The longer I went on starting businesses, writing books and jet-setting around, the further the gap grew.

People from my youth kept coming up to me like, "Heather, stop this bullshit. Get married and find a fun house to raise a bunch of kids in."

They missed me at bible study and out on the lake on the 4th of July.

But I knew I couldn't go back to living that old life no more.

Sometimes we simply have to make adjustments and revolutions for our life. For our freedom. For our being. To get the most out of it for ourselves and for our loved ones.

What we give attention to grows. If we want to grow something profitable and good, we have to put our time into it. If you really want to walk the entrepreneurial road, find space to take care of you.

I've been through my share of relationships and for a long time I struggled to not make "my man" the biggest priority in my life. I made the girlfriend-y mistake over and over before I learned my lesson; I focused too much on my lovers, placing their wants and needs before my own.

I paid heavily for those mistakes.

I know now that if I take care of myself first—health, finances, business—then I am better equipped to take care of others.

Carve out the time for yourself. When you nurture yourself, you are better equipped to help others.

So, make sure to create energy and space just for you.

For, taking care of yourself is not narcissistic. It is loving yourself.

Prioritize yourself and prioritize your business. All too often I see my clients treating their business like a side hustle—too often because they just don't believe they have the time for it.

I had this client: mid-40s, divorced, with a ten-year-old son. She hired me because she said she wanted to have "a real business" so she could quit her day job.

However, she admitted that she had been so intent on "being mommy" that she hadn't been focused enough on the business. She was "afraid of thinking big," she told me.

We worked together for a while. She told me it was going to take a lot of time and a lot of energy to transition from "mommy" to "Mama Bear."

But she did.

She UnCaged in a big way. And now she is making a lot more money. And her kids have a life of a lot more freedom. And so does she.

UnCaged Lesson:

A life of ultimate freedom is a choice.

CORE VS. CONFUSION.

To thrive in the entrepreneurial game, you have to be confident in your core message.

So, how do we do this?

Well, confidence comes through clarity; through crystal clear clarity in *what* you are doing, in *why* you are doing it, and in *who* you are doing it for. Because...

"A Confused Mind Never Buys."

Get confident in your core message and clear on your ideal client. Do this and the sales will come.

To get this confidence and charisma flowing, you need three parts: your message, your media, and your market.

Your Message: What is the problem you are solving for your Market?

Your Market: Who is Your Market? What is their Biggest Problem? What is their Biggest Challenge?

Your Media: The Media is where you will be sharing and selling your message to your market.

You gotta be absolutely one hundred percent clear on who you are and what your brand stands for.

Write out who your market is. Name them; write out precisely what your target market looks like, feels like, what they drool over, what keeps them up at night, what they fear.

Write out what different types of media you want to use first. podcast, social media, YouTube. Brainstorm it. Envision it. Make it happen.

Once you've done this, then go to all of your social media profiles and have the same personal brand image across all platforms. Your bio and your links to your offers, make them all congruent; because if you are out of sync on any of your platforms—if you appear one way in one place and a different way in some other place—you'll lose trust. You'll lose trust by confusing people.

Why?

Because a confused mind never buys.

Oh, and be attractive.

No, I'm not talking about showing some leg, I'm talking about being attractive to your target market.

You become attractive by exuding that confidence we just talked about. Consumers are attracted to people who are convicted about what they are doing, attracted to people who have conviction in what they are talking about—attracted to people who *inspire*.

So, when you speak, speak with authority. This doesn't mean be a jerk, it means don't be wishy-washy. It means speak with a clarity of message, a distinct and clear value-add, and with a powerful call to action.

Communicate that:

1) You are the expert and the authority to your target market

2) You are clear on the problem they have

3) You are confident in how you will solve it

To help get your message heard, there are four types of content to use: audio, video, images, and written word.

Stick to your strengths here. If you love the camera, then do a ton of videos. If you have a radio voice but don't like the lights, focus on podcasting and social audio platforms.

My natural strengths are in speaking and in being in front of the camera, so, as I built my empire I focused on audio and video. As I continue to create content as much as I can, I've expanded into the written word in blogs and books.

And images? Though the market is moving away from static images, they still play—but only if you do them well, which probably means only if you like doing them.

My advice is to pick the two types of content you are best at and double down on them, especially if you are just starting out. Stick to what you're good at. I start my clients out with a podcast. I find that a podcast is the easiest and fastest way to create content and increase your visibility, authority, and online reach. Try it out.

UnCaged Lesson:

Get clear on your core message—and then get it out there, confidently.

Audience

SEE IT FOR WHAT IT IS

I know more than a few women and a couple of men who are so caged by their home, caged by their "success," comfortably numbed by their walls and their things, that they no longer have the drive to go out and do more. I call that being 'in the drift of the cage.'

I can see it in them. I know the feeling because I grew up that way.

I don't remember much about my young childhood, but I remember we had a nice house. Supposedly my father made a lot of money. My parents could entertain and show off with the best of 'em. They had cool things and made the space to put them in.

But that house lacked connection. It lacked human connection. After my father left, that house became my Cage.

My sister sequestered herself off in a locked-up wing of the house, and I converted a Jack n' Jill bedroom into my dwelling.

It was a cage of isolation, a cage of the façade of a great life, a cage that prevented me from becoming the Heather I needed to become for a long time.

However, at that time I felt comfortable in my cage; because I couldn't *see* it. It was just the 'way it was.'

That's why so many cages exist all around us. Oftentimes they become so ingrained that they become invisible. And we must first become aware of the iron bars of our cage before we can rip them open.

So, bad-ass UnCager, I ask you to look around your life. What may have become so ingrained that it has become invisible? What may be a cage in your life that you do not yet see?

How are you gonna see it? And how are you gonna rip it wide open?

When I was first UnCaging, I looked to a book for help: Dr. Joe Dispensa's *Breaking the Habit of Being Yourself*.

I love this book. Plus, it has a ton of amazing meditations that sync up with it and its lessons. One of the main messages is to Break the Habit of your old ways. You do this by being open to the reality that the "you" that you call yourself is not really you—but merely the longest-standing habit of your life.

I *was* that habit. I was told as a teenager that I was shy and stupid, so I acted shy and stupid. That was a habit and that was a cage. Then I was told I did not have any value outside of my body, so I acted like the only value I had to offer the world was my body. That was a habit and that was a cage.

Before I UnCaged, I was miserable. I attracted abusive relationships. My whole life was one big bad habit. I had to learn how to break the habit of being "myself." Only then would I see the real me.

Maybe it has or will be the same, for you.

UnCaged Lesson:

Numbness to the cage is the cage. Break the habit. Now.

THE GUIDE SAYS "GO DEEPER"

I went to a retreat once. To go on a journey, of the ancient kind. The kind that gets your brain and your soul into a primal place of awakening. It was a modern vision-quest weekend, and I drank the magical tea.

There were about twenty other people, a mix of business people, entrepreneurs, hippies, and those in between. We came to seek. We drank and we waited for the purge and it came. Our stomachs told our brain to purge of the toxins and bad juju—twenty adults sitting cross-legged, puking like kindergarteners.

And then came the healing. On came the clarity, the purity, the perspective and the wisdom.

Things got clear.

Hours passed.

At one point, the guide walked over to me. "Would you like to go deeper?" he asked.

Childlike, I responded with a "yes" or a "yeah" or a "why not." I am not sure. But I am sure what happened next.

I went deeper.

Deeper into my past, deeper into my future, deeper into my present. *The* present. The one, true, all-seeing present.

And it was a gift.

Then this dreadlocked girl, a co-traveler with me on the journey, asked me out of the void, "So your brand's called again, *UnCage*?"

"Yes, it is."

She tilted her head curiously. "So, when are *you* going to UnCage?"

I looked at her, still childlike, still curious; clear, pure.

And it hit me.

Though I knew I had UnCaged a great deal in my life, at that moment I knew I could UnCage more—do more, be freer, be more curious, bolder.

I looked at the dreadlocked girl and answered her question. "Always," I said. "I will *always* be UnCaging."

"Me too," she said.

And we both laughed.

UnCaged Lesson:

Journeys lead you home.

AUDIENCE OWNERSHIP.

Whmen you're dealing with any kind of brand or any sort of marketing, you have to focus on your audience, right? You Better!

But what type of audience?

Clients. And there are three types of clients to focus on: Buyers, Peers, and the Brand Audience.

Let's dive in.

Your Buyers: the people whom your business is solving a problem for. These are the people who are going to put money straight into your business bank account. They are the most important part of your business. Get connected to them, get intimate with your buyer.

When I say "get intimate," I don't mean date them, I mean really get inside their head—their desires, their pain, their needs, their challenges. Get to know them inside and out.

I even sometimes place an image of my buyer along with their name next to my desk so I know who I am speaking to when I write that blog post or host that live room or do that LIVE.

For my mentorship program, for instance, one of my buyers is a woman named Jane. She is 45, smart, savvy, into learning about tech, and desires to have her business reach a consistent six figures so she can leave her old job. She's doing it. She's UnCaging. And it doesn't look like she'll have to stay at the old job anymore to feel financially secure. Plus, her new business is projecting a ton of direct impact on people's lives. Jane feels more fulfilled—like we all do when we rip off some layers of the onion and take a crowbar to the cage.

I know I've said this before, but it bears restating: hone in on your target market—know everything you can about them.

Get super-ultra-mega specific on this. Go deep. Is your target market male or female? Old or young? Straight or LGBT? Kids or no kids? Do they own a beat-up pickup truck or a shiny red Audi? Are they brunch people or do they eat three boiled eggs and a banana in the same kitchen chair every morning?

The key to audience ownership is focusing on the miniature characteristics of exactly who will benefit from your product or service.

And remember, these aren't your fans or followers; they are your buyers—the people in your audience that you need to convert to sales. Period.

Your Peers: Even as a solo entrepreneur, and maybe *especially* as a solo entrepreneur, you have to build a team.

This may sound counterintuitive, but it is essential. Business is a team sport. The faster you build a team, the faster you will make money. One of the biggest mistakes I made early in my entrepreneurial life was not playing "team." I treated business like golf rather than a team sport.

Like in football—love the game or hate it, it is a fact that a good play requires all eleven people on the field to do their job and work together. The quarterback cannot both throw the ball *and* catch the ball. A running back cannot run for a touchdown without the linemen blocking for him.

In your solopreneuring, you won't be able to play every position. Learn and play the positions you are best at—doing what you are good at— and then outsource and get mentorship for the other parts. I call it "cutting a check for speed." I have invested over a million dollars in the last two decades in my education, with mentors, and personal development (*not* including college).

Entrepreneurship is about constantly investing in yourself—to enhance yourself, to grow your business, and to scale and leverage your time. Invest in the right mentors, the right communities, and the right people. It's really not that hard to do. Reach out to your peers on social media, comment on people's posts, attend other people's events, pick up the phone and ask how someone's day is.

Be proactive with your peers. A little give goes a long way.

Brand Audience: This is the group of people that are your followers but not necessarily your buyers. This audience is a little more nuanced, and the way it works best is to think with the end in mind, the end being: what kind of brands do you want to write your checks for you?

Think like this and work backward. Figure out who and what you align with, and go attract them. Create content for them and engage with them.

Think of it like the girl or hunk you wanted to date back in high school; you knew who they were *before* you started wooing them. It's the same with business—know your goal, know who you want to kiss at the end of the dance, and work your butt off to get them dancing. This is where your short-form video, your podcast interviews, and your LIVES really begin to matter.

For finding and reaching your ideal audience—for finding and reaching your ideal target market—I encourage, plain and simple, nothing less than domination. More specifically, what I call iDomm: Influence Domination.

Got a nice ring, huh?

I think so too, that's why I trademarked it. It means "being omnipresent, being everywhere at once. Being always and ever."

iDomm means creating content that is as evergreen as possible and continually repurposing it across all your handles and avenues, all the time.

In this sense, your job is to get noticed and garner engagement by your brand audience as desired by your target audience. To do this, strive to be like God. I'm not trying to be blasphemous here, I'm just saying "be everywhere." The more places you are, the more people will find you.

I tell my students to not discriminate where people want to consume their content. With me, for example, just because I do not like Twitter, it does not mean I don't post on Twitter.

Influence, through Domination and by being Everywhere. Do this because the more a person or brand consumes you—the more content of yours they digest—the easier and faster and more frequently they will click "buy now."

It's like that girl or guy at the end of the dance; they'll be a lot more likely to kiss you if they've already spent time with you in school. The kiss comes a lot easier after they've consumed some of your personality and authenticity.

It's the same with being an UnCaged Entrepreneur. And our consumption is multifaceted: it's the audio, video, image, and written word we talked about earlier. So get on it. Mastery of content creation is critical for your brand. Make your brand a plate that is desirable and ready to be eaten. Make people want you. Attract people toward you.

Solo entrepreneurship ain't 'the oldest profession' but it also ain't that different. It's all sales.

Your audience wants to know what you sound like. Give it to them. Be yourself from the first second. It takes people less than ten minutes of listening to a podcast to decide if they like you or not—and sometimes a few seconds is all we have to make an impression.

Get as much content out there as you possibly can. And then give free samples. Give little appetizers. When their hunger can no longer be satisfied by bits and pieces, they'll buy the whole thing.

Let's go deeper:

There is another key differentiation when it comes to building an audience: "leasing" an audience and "owning" your audience.

When you're engaging through social media, you are *leasing* your audience. But to get where you want to go, you must eventually own your audience. When you move people from social media into your email list, community group, or as a subscriber to your podcast, you are *owning* your audience.

And the value of your business is determined by what you own. For your audience, that is growing your list—getting people off social media and putting them into what I call your "GDP." Not your Gross Domestic Product, your Groups-Database-Pages.

Groups-Database-Pages is your email list. It's taking your audience to pages that you own so you can get data from them. You can pixel them for future retargeting and get more of their data.

We all know that data is one of the big currencies of the new paradigm. So, own your media and leverage it to own your audience. Don't just grow your followers; grow your ability and capacity to grow your "list."

Meet your audience on social media or on the street—and then get them into your GDPs.

A little business lesson from Trump here. Hate him or love him, he's done some smart things in business—some things that have helped him when things went south. Like when he was pulled off Twitter and lost eighty-seven million followers. That's a huge number to lose.

Thing is, he'd been building his email list and text message list for years. He'd been diligent as hell about it because he knew how important owning his audience was. So, even though he "lost" those eighty-seven million followers, he really didn't. Within a month after the Twitter ban he was already back to spreading his influence and receiving donations at the level he was before the ban, all because he understood the principles of this book and owned his data.

Another example: One that didn't work out so well, about a business coach and friend of mine.

She was and is a super successful coach who had her Facebook account hacked. It wasn't her fault, but Zuckerberg still shut her down; her personal page, her business page, everything.

She lost fifteen years' worth of friends, pictures, messages, groups, followers, audience members, and potential buyers. In one day, it was all gone.

Everything she had built was gone, vanished—and unfortunately, she hadn't "backed up" her audience. She hadn't built the email list. And she had to start her coaching business from scratch, because she had still been just 'leasing' her audience.

Don't let this happen to you.

UnCaged Lesson:

Influence Domination = Impact and Income

Genuine

DRAGON GODDESS

The words "wizard" and "witch" have always fascinated me. Which one has a more positive connotation to you?

What's the first image that pops into your head when I say "wizard?" When I say "witch?"

For most of us, the term wizard conjures (pun intended) the positive image of some old guy with a long white beard. Merlin or Gandalf or something. And witch? Well, most Americans picture a green-skinned mole-ridden shrew riding a broom.

That's because those are the definitions, and images, that have been thrust upon us. However, in the dictionary form, the words mean the same thing—simply with different genders attached to the definitions. A wizard is a "male wizard," and a witch is a "female wizard."

In our modern verbiage, someone can be a "wizard" at math or a "wiz" at the piano. These are compliments. Try calling someone a witch—and if you're not at Burning Man, watch out.

Wizard connotates a wise person and a witch connotates being a bitch or an evil person.

Even when we get to the historical witches, let's take some of those witch trials of the 1600s. Do you know what a lot of those "witches" were accused of? Dancing. Yep. Some of the first "witches" of that New England town were a few teenage girls—no doubt bored out of their minds at the Puritanical culture in which they were living—who thought it would be fun to go out into the forest under the light of the full moon and dance.

And they were accused of witchcraft and tried as witches,

I don't remember that happening to Kevin Bacon in *Footloose*.

Those girls had a cage put on them. A colossal one or, I suppose, a super small one depending on how you see it.

Fast forward to the 2020s and society, the world even, is opening up a lot. Feminine energy is rising. Look at all the female-driven movies coming out. Look at the women who are making it into the highest ranks of politics.

The earth is female. Gaia. We've always called it *Mother* Earth. There was a time when matriarchal societies were common—it was back before the ancient Greeks of the Iliad and the Odyssey, led by a people known as the Minoans and commonly referred to as the *Pax Mediterranea*. These peaceful Mediterranean cultures worshipped beautiful "Earth Goddesses" rather than the warlike "Sky Gods" of the cultures who took them over and handed us a patriarchal society.

I find it interesting to think about. I wonder what, how, and why that market was valued back then?

Sometimes, my fascination for witches and wizards and magic becomes too great and I have to do something about it.

So, on December 21, 2020, the winter solstice, and the oldest pagan holiday out there, some of my friends and I got together.

We were sitting in a darkened room, a pyramid with an open ceiling to the moon and stars. The structure was built over flowing water. It was amazing. And we weren't allowed to bring our phones or computers. No tech. We were only allowed to bring our bodies and minds/souls.

And we started chanting, and doing breathwork. Our faces were lit only by candles as we worked with sound bowls and all sorts of stuff. In time, we began chanting louder and then screaming like crazy. If someone had walked in on us, it would have looked like seance from a movie.

I was getting my Dragon Goddess on. That night I was referred to as "Your Rebel Highness."

So, what were we doing?

We were reactivating our crystalline DNA. Getting in tune. Reconnecting to the wisdom of our primordial roots.

A lot of people from the Cage of my life would say it looked like witchcraft. I call it getting super-connected to the universe. Tapping in. Getting centered.

See, society is dictated by what is popular *right now*. When the Stonewall Riots happened in 1969 and gay men were beaten in the streets, homosexuality was not very popular. When lynching occurred throughout the South in the days of Jim Crow, being black was not very popular. When women were told to stay at home to cook and clean, a woman going out and making something of herself in the marketplace was not very popular.

But it's changing. The world is UnCaging. And revolutions are waged with ideas as much as bombs.

So, wizard vs. witch; homemaker vs. entrepreneur; corporate America vs. everyone becoming their own CEO, change is upon us. It is happening. It is here. We are taking our power as we UnCage, one person at a time, to create the world we envision. A world where we can dance in the forest and not be called a witch. A world where we can embrace who we are and know that it's enough. A world where people and the market respect difference and uniqueness.

Know this: in one of its oldest definitions, the word "weird" means "spiritual." Probably because the spiritual folk in the days of the old rocked the boat of established norms. Just like UnCaged Entrepreneurs. To be weird meant "different," and to be "different" meant "spiritual."

So I suppose Jesus and his early followers were "weird."

My point is that weird things can gain momentum. Oprah is weird. Beyonce is weird. Madonna, yeah, she's definitely weird.

And it is "weird" that moves the world.

UnCaged Lesson:

Be a wizard and embrace your witch. The world will thank you.

EVERYTHING IS CONNECTED TO EVERYTHING ELSE

It was seven days before the presidential election of 2020 and the world was jacked up. I was driving down the road, and I had to take the left onto the freeway that I'd done a thousand times—but the guy behind me won't let me over!

To stop my car from hitting the median, I have to abruptly pull my SUV onto the side of the road. I almost drove right into the ditch.

Then the guy drives by me with his arms flailing, flipping me off and cussing at me. And I'm on the side of the road in my car just thinking, "the world is losing it."

To that guy, maybe it was.

And it affected me.

Because everything that happens around us affects us. You've heard of the butterfly effect, right? So, yeah, the stock market affects us. What China does affects us. How our neighbor celebrates their holidays affects us. Everything does.

One little example: oranges.

I eat an orange every single day. Love 'em. They taste good, my doctor friend tells me how good they are for digestion, and they give me a little boost of energy. I like them.

So, one day early in the pandemic I went to the grocery store to get my oranges. I take them home, all happy to eat them over the next week or so, but the very next day I saw mold on them!

I was bummed, but chalked it up as a bad apple (orange) and went to a different grocery store. Same thing; I took them home and they were moldy by the next day.

The next day, I went to a different store. Same thing—moldy friggin' oranges, within one or two days of buying them.

I knew my world had changed but up until that point, I had yet to understand to what extent. A virus had turned the world on its side and because of it my oranges were moldy.

Yep, everything is connected. In life and in business. The key is to UnCage our perspective so we may understand why—and how—the interconnected ripples affect us.

Only then can we begin to shift and be 100% responsible for EVERYTHING in our lives. Everything is a frequency, a vibration—and we get to choose what we place our focus and energy on.

You want a great life? Then focus your vibration, your frequency, on gratitude and creating an UnCaged Business and Life.

UnCaged Lesson:

Vibrations are Real.

LABELS

I stopped drinking on December 31, 2019. I had just read a book called *The Naked Mind*, and it was about not putting anything into your brain that blurs your clarity. I was trying to rebuild my business (again), my life (always), and the UnCaged brand, so I decided to give up alcohol. It is a depressant, after all, and I needed all of me.

In my life at that time, even though things on the outside looked great, on the inside it wasn't working. So, I went to Christmas dinner and told my sister, "I'm not drinking."

She freaked out (we're a drinking family) and she promptly called the waiter over and ordered me a glass of wine. I reluctantly sipped at it during our dinner but wasn't into it.

I floated the idea of drinking vs. not drinking for the week, and that New Year's Eve I decided to go to a bar and have a glass of champagne and dance with some strangers.

It was fun until it wasn't.

I looked at my phone. It was 11:15. Forty-five minutes left in the year; forty-five minutes left in the decade.

"As good a time as ever," I said out loud after I swigged the last sip of my glass of champagne.

I walked outside and hopped in a cab, and that was it for me and alcohol.

I'm so glad I did it. It was a real uncaging moment for me and my relationship with my body. Not only my physical body but my emotional body too—my thoughts toward my body, my feelings about my body, and how to relate to being a woman in her 40s.

Stopping drinking started a lot for me. I stopped the self-inflicted pain that drinking caused my emotional and physical states.

And in all honesty, I don't think I could have come as far as I did in one year if alcohol was still a part of my life. I couldn't have healed as much. I couldn't have UnCaged as much.

See, I've always had a lot of issues regarding my body image. Again, not just the physical but the emotional and spiritual body and how it all relates to the six inches between my ears.

I was a hardcore bodybuilder for a long time, and when I was doing that shit—up on the stage with my ass looking perfect and my stomach rippling with abs—you know what, that was the unhealthiest I was in my entire life.

It was such a grind to get "competition ready," such a bullshit regiment we'd put ourselves through. We'd do all sorts of terrible things to our bodies for months so we could have our one day up on stage.

For what? A ribbon? A plastic trophy? So the judges could critique us?

And then I'd go out six months later and actually be eating properly again. I'd show someone a picture of me from the competition, and they'd be like, "wow, that's *you?*"

In the photo, my skin would be like seven shades darker from all the tanning; I'd have so much makeup on, I'd have not had a carb in a month or drank water in days. They'd barely recognize me. Because that photo was not me. Not the *real* me.

It's a weird world, bodybuilding.

What you have to realize is the people on stage don't look like that for three hundred and sixty-five days a year. They look like that once or twice a year, three times a year maybe, but not all year round; not bodybuilders or pageant queens or Derek Zoolander.

Before I got out of the bodybuilding world, I would regularly see a chiropractor because of the pains in my lower back and spine.

"You look great," he'd say to me, "but your body is not healthy. Let's start with your endocrine system. . ."

And he'd give me these lectures about energy and health and western medicine and eastern science, highlighting all that I was not doing right for my body.

Lesson: We all judge a book by its cover. We *all* do. Just don't do it with your body. I've been there. It's not a fun read.

I used to say, "I love going to the gym!"

Well, that was not accurate. I was *addicted* to going to the gym—to the social aspect, to the "look how great I look" aspect, to the competition of me-against-the-other-physical-bodies-around-me aspect.

Back then, I would look at someone who was overweight, and my ego would tell me, "You're better than that person," and I'd get this hit of dopamine.

It was bad. I see that now. I didn't see it then. It took a total shift of mind frame. A totally different sight. A lot of UnCaging.

Similar to why I stopped drinking.

Both were big cages for me. Sure, those glasses of wine in the evening made me feel good. But just like the ego boost from being more physically fit than someone, it was fake.

See, on many levels, I know I am an addict. A lot of entrepreneurs are. We get into something, and we just keep doing it. It can become us. Consume us.

Part of our journey in being a solo entrepreneur is about finding positive outlets for our energies. The research on addiction will tell you that it is usually a sign of running away from something. I know I was running away from a lot of trauma for a long dang time. When I was thirteen months old, my mom was stabbed seventeen times and assaulted by a stranger. Attempted murder. In our home. In the middle of a summer day. I was in the house with her.

I do somehow remember a few pieces of the assault.

It was beyond traumatic.

She survived, physically, but there was nothing else left. Her trauma manifested as disconnection. I won't go into detail except to say that she got disconnected from herself to such a degree that, energetically, she became incapable of being a parent to her child.

That child was me. So I went inward. I stopped talking. No words. For a long time.

Top that off with being sexually abused as a 5-year-old and, yeah, there were some things going on in me that I've had to break free from.

Research tells us that the ADD brain is a brain that is trying to survive—not focusing deeply on things but scattering, constantly responding to stimuli in an attempt to stay busy.

Needless to say, in 1981, before it was a widely known and accepted thing, I was diagnosed with ADD.

And then that label of my life really started to kick into high gear. I would constantly be hearing the words: "There's something wrong with Heather."

I'd be playing with pots on the floor when my mom had friends over, and I would hear her whisper to them. I always hated how they didn't think I could hear them. But I could. I *did*. "There's something wrong with Heather." That label. I heard it over and over and internalized the message.

It didn't help that mom threw me into all these tests. Tests in cold rooms with metal chairs and wires coming out of my head. Random stranger-nurses, me, and these tests.

For hours.

I started to really, truly believe that there was "something wrong with me." I mean, I knew my friends weren't spending *their* Saturdays like this.

And then came the diagnosis: attention deficit disorder. All I heard was "disorder."

Boom. Another label.

I began to believe in the labels put on me. I thought something *really was* wrong with me. I thought I was this bad apple or something.

Mom lived with a sort of "Heather's never gonna make it" type attitude, and it must have rubbed off on me. I wore it. Fuck. For way too long.

In school, I had to go to this special area where they gave me "medicine" (yeah, it was Ritalin), and I had to have all these meetings with the teachers all the time.

I was a special case, and everyone knew it. Especially me.

Even though I eventually did start talking, it led to me being in speech therapy for seven years (never could say spaghetti) and left me without the confidence to participate verbally in anything when I was young.

I maintained my isolation. And I stayed there. I never spoke in class. I mean *never*. I wouldn't even raise my hand. (Maybe it's why I talk so much now.)

Because for a big part of my adult life, my daily mission was to prove to all the haters that "Fuck you, nothing's wrong with me!"

I sought out attention. I craved being behind the camera. I got drunk and talked loudly. I slept with people I didn't want to because I thought I should and felt it would get me attention. I did what I thought other people would want me to do. I sought outside validation.

And, for decades, that was the Cage I lived in.

The key that took me out from that cage? Becoming an entrepreneur.

I remember hearing the word for the first time: en-tre-pren-eur. It was this magic word.

But when I looked into the magic word it had a very real definition: a person who organizes and manages any enterprise, especially in business, usually with a considerable initiative.

I was like, okay, this is for me. This is my outlet. This is where I can put my energy, let loose, make money, be who I am. This is where the nerds can be themselves. Even the ones with blonde hair and big boobs.

I started doing everything entrepreneurial under the sun. I'd go to meet-ups and started hanging out with a bunch of entrepreneurs who were really doing it—and they were all crazy.

They were all a bit off (*we* were all a bit off), and we were finding ways to use our "off-ness" to create cool things and make money.

Becoming an entrepreneur was great. It got me out of a cage.

I did a lot.

I made a lot of money.

I created.

But, over time, it became just another cage. Because I wasn't doing it for the right 'why.' I was doing it to prove something about the preexisting cage. I initially became an entrepreneur to prove that I was enough; it was simply a secondary manifestation of the first cage.

It took me a few years before I started being an entrepreneur for me, from me. And I still walk that path every day. A lot of my path is about realizing that none of the labels put on me during my life were right— that they weren't even close and that they weren't even real. There wasn't anything wrong with me. I just do things my own way. Like we all should do.

In a universal market where all is one, where all is connected and interconnected, a label isn't even really a real thing. Because everything is flowing and moving all the time, uniquely its own.

Or it should be.

When we start breaking down the labels, we start breaking down the cage; and we become better entrepreneurs and better people.

UnCaged Lesson:

People will label you. Don't allow yourself to accept it.

GENUINE RELATIONSHIPS.

Even though a lot of us are weird, potentially-eccentric, solo-type entrepreneurs, the best way to build what we want to build is to do it with other people. Relationships.

I know, it can sound scary. It was for me.

Early on in my career, I held myself back because I treated business relationships like some annoying necessary evil rather than the giving them proper time and respect. That was a cage for me for a long time, at least until I thought about it and did an about-face. I looked it the mirror and knew I had to change. I could no longer deny that *who* we know matters at least as much as *what* we know. There is an innate 'power in the group' for the solopreneur: if people are working with you, it shows both you and others that you have a good idea and a solid plan of action.

And that says a lot.

If you're the lone wolf, people will tend to guard their treasures from you. Trust will be hard to get. I know. For a long time I was that lone wolf who caused people to stand back a bit. I absolutely hated hearing the fucking phrase, "It's not what you know, but who you know."

I hated it until I came to *understand* it, came to see it for what it actually means. It's not nepotism. It's building networks—because who you know adds to your authority. It really does.

So, why does it matter more *who* you know than *what* you know? Because people don't buy quality, they buy what they know; people buy their connections.

Thus, authority doesn't stem solely from an idea or an invention; it comes from the combination of what you create and who you know to help spread the word.

So, to get a whole bunch of creation going, I encourage you to seek out and create strategic partnerships. To get them, it's pretty easy: simply give something of yourself. Help out other entrepreneurs. Go on their podcasts. Give some free coaching. Help with a design or do some writing work for them. Say "yes."

Doing so basically amps up your relationship currency bank account. It's putting a payment down that you can later withdraw from. That's how friendship works, and so that's how business works.

Symbiotically.

Last week, for example, I moved some things around in my schedule so I could devote an hour of my time to help a strategic partner with her product launch.

I went online with her because we both knew I could help her sales. She knew this. I knew this. And I know she has her zone of genius that will help me someday down the line in one of my ventures. I know we are there for each other. Like strategic partners. Like friends.

We both know that we live symbiotically, that each of our businesses are better off when helped out by the other.

Have you ever seen chimpanzees grooming each other on some Planet Earth type show? Yeah, they do it all the time, picking ticks and sticks and dirt from each other's coats. The behavior is an absolute staple of chimpanzee social structure. It helps build bonds. It brings individuals closer, because grooming someone else's coat helps ensure you don't have a dirty coat yourself. It's a symbiotic act. It's a 'give to receive.'

So, for example, if you want to get onto podcasts but aren't getting the invite, start your own podcast and invite people to be on yours. That will open the flow.

Invite, and you will be invited.

Even if you are not a social person (let's face it, a lot of us just aren't), give yourself some 'stretch marks' by going out of your comfort zone to engage with others and build strategic partnerships.

To do this well, we all have to learn to navigate egos. Both other people's and our own.

I find that this is best done through talking little and listening a lot. Listen to what the human being is saying and how they are saying it. Think about your responses more so than just reacting to what they say.

On your entrepreneurship journey, you will do business with people of different religious and political beliefs to you. You will form strategic partnerships with people who like country music; you will form strategic partnerships with people who like rap music; and you will form strategic partnerships with people who like salsa music.

Learn to appreciate what others appreciate; there are 8,000,000,000+ billion of us on this planet. That's a lot of egos. One way to do this is to embrace what Todd Herman calls "The Alter Ego Effect."

Todd is a cutting-edge entrepreneur and author, and business associate. Like me, he likes to make sports references in relation to business. He talks about how when an athlete puts on his or her uniform, that athlete becomes another piece of themselves. Kobe Bryant (R.I.P.) was a rather quiet dude off the court.

But when he put on his Los Angeles Laker uniform, he turned into an absolute intensity machine. Putting on the yellow and purple jersey and lacing up his sneakers, Kobe Bryant became "The Black Mamba." His persona changed, and it was time for him *to go to work.*

As entrepreneurs, we should strive to achieve this effect too. Find a way to get your 'game face' on when you are on the call or in the office.

Like Kobe, it can be through some sort of uniform (maybe it's a certain red tie or your 'pink power panties'). Maybe it's a pin you put on or a certain necklace. A pair of power shoes? A pair of rad sunglasses?

Or maybe it's just the look in your eye.

Always be authentic, yes, but don't be afraid to have a couple of personas. An athlete is not the same person at game time as they are at lunchtime, and neither should you. You should probably not interact with every person you meet in the same way. Some human beings will require more humility on your part. Some may necessitate more bravado. We are, as Aristotle called us, "political animals."

So get your game face on, read the defense, and make a play.

In entrepreneurship, you are a creator, a businessperson, an athlete, a psychologist, and a politician. Not necessarily in that order.

And every day is different.

UnCaged Lesson:

The ability to create partnerships makes the solopreneur thrive.

Ease

TRIBE UP AND APPLY

I've never been a big fan of Christmas. No, I'm not talking about the nativity and the Christian stuff or even fake-flocked trees. I'm talking about the Christmas that begins the day after Halloween. I'm talking about Walmart aisles. I'm talking about the month-and-a-half long advertising campaign that society has accepted. I'm talking about the television commercials and the internet ads of happy families smiling with their two-and-a-half kids and the picket fence—and how it gives this image that, if your family doesn't look like this you've somehow messed up.

Well, *that's* messed up. Because it's not true.

If you look back at history, back to our hunter-gatherer and tribal times, you'll learn how we evolved to be brought up in a *community*. How it truly "took a village." How we weren't the possessions of our moms or dads because we were part of 'The Tribe.'

When we got out of that and into a more structured society, let's say the times of kings and queens, we can literally read the history books to see how many times people killed off a family member to rise. You see, even though family is great, it's not always (or even often) a community of like-minded people. That's why we sometimes have to go out and create our own family. We can still go back home every once in a while, but we can (and sometimes need to) also go out and form new partnerships. Because when you start UnCaging in life and business, all of a sudden you get to choose *who* your brothers and sisters are. You get to create your own T.R.I.B.E.

And there is power in that. It comes down to choice. For when we equip ourselves to *choose* rather than settle, that's when the ideas really start rolling. That's when the cross-mojonation and cross-pollination start flowing.

When we UnCage from those we *have* to be with—whether it's family or old friends or our current shitty boss—we often free ourselves to be ourselves.

When we UnCage our mind, we change our energy. When we change our energy, we change what we attract. When we change what we attract, we wake up and find ourselves in the Tribe—around and among the people we want to be with.

Which is the best and only place to be to expand yourself.

I spent a good part of my life thinking something was wrong with me because I didn't fit the Hallmark card idea. Well, it took me a while in life to understand that something *is* wrong with the Hallmark card idea that's pushed upon us.

Someone once told me, "Heather, you did not travel all this way to 'play small.'"

I jived with it. I am here to play big. I live every day with those words in mind. I believe in reincarnation (fascinating stuff, lots to read up on there), and I understand that I came a long way to get here. You did too, to get into this body, in this time, on this earth.

You and I are both part of the grand cosmos, and we must go for it while we can.

My biggest fear is that I'm lying in the nursing home and my best friend Kym looks down at me and says, "did you do everything you wanted to do in this life?" and that I can't say "yes" to her question.

That's my nightmare, and so I try to *live* my highest and best self—free from all old constraints.

I've been envisioning this book being a bestseller for over two years. That's my big picture. That's me not playing small. By the time you're reading this, maybe it is. Maybe it's not there yet. But I am here for the big game—in this book, in my business, in my relationships. In everything I do.

So, yeah, I believe that it took a lot for each of us to travel the universe to get into this body in this time in this place. We don't know where or when we'll get our next earth kit. So let's UnCage, live large, and make the most of our time on this planet.

●•▬—•—▬●▬—•—▬•●

I tell friends and clients who are struggling to break open their cage, "You've had the keys with you the entire time. It is about time you start using them."

It's true. The keys to unlocking our cage are within our possession. Always have been. We just have to locate them.

For instance, I was telling this woman about winning my Stevie Award. I told her that the reason I won, at its core, was "because I applied." Because I filled out the application and put myself out there.

She looked at me, nodded, and then started telling me about this award in Austin that she'd always wanted.

"So, have you applied?" I ask.

"Well, no," she says.

"Well, you can't win if you don't apply!"

And she had this big "aha" look on her face. It was great. We talked a bit more, and she said she was going to finally do it. She would finally overcome her fear of judgment and fill out her application for the award she'd always wanted.

Yep.

And guess what? She called me up a couple days after that conversation, telling me how she'd picked up the magazine, filled it out the application and submitted it.

"Nice!" I told her.

She gave herself the chance, and she's got a great shot at the award.

All because she applied.

If you don't apply, things stay the same. And things "staying the same" is not what UnCaging is about. UnCaging is about breaking free from the norm to transform. To take charge of our life. To wake up and break free from what's been pushed upon us. To challenge ourselves.

But this only happens when we elevate above the worry of being judged, fill out the application, and take the bold steps to make life happen.

The world is far from perfect. The world of business is far from perfect. But they've both got a lot of potential. And each of us can help it get better. A lot better. By finding our Tribe and allowing ourselves to apply.

You didn't come all this way to play small.

Don't settle. Play big.

FUNNELS AND MENTORS AND GUIDES

Back in 1999 I was working for a big Fortune 500 company in Fort Worth, Texas. Not Dallas, not Houston, Fort Worth; which was pretty much considered the red-headed stepchild of Dallas. But I didn't care. I was 24 years old, and I was making moves in outside sales. All of my co-workers were men over 40 supporting their wives and kids. I really wasn't supposed to be there. There were no other 24-year-old females around. I was the company test tube, put there to see if I could survive.

Nowadays "funnels" are all over the place—you know, the email chains and all those pages on a website automating a customer through the platform. They're pretty much ubiquitous to online marketing in the 2020s, but in '99 it wasn't like that.

Well, long story short, I figured out how to make one.

My target audience was a very large military company. (One you may have heard of.)

I knew they had money to spend, and I knew everyone on the payroll had an email. I also knew that they had a fax machine. That was enough for me to make a plan.

I sent fifteen emails out to the company of about thirty thousand employees, a simple email stating: "Here's a special offer for your company. Please share it with your co-workers."

Then I attached a simple but snazzy one-page flyer.

And I hit send.

Well, they must have used that fax machine and those email addresses to funnel my message around the office. Because the very next Monday there was a stack of papers on my desk, my email inbox was filled up, and there were orders for me on the fax tray.

Dozens upon dozens of them.

It was the same the next day. And the next. I'm talking *stacks*.

So I knew I had my funnel. It worked very well, so good that it basically started to run itself and I barely had to work. The invoices were flowing.

So all I really had to do was come into the office from about ten 'til two, see how big my stacks were, process the orders, and then go home to work on college homework (oh, yeah, I went to university at night too).

Then I got a call one day at the office. "Heather, you are in The Winners Circle. Our company has over ten thousand reps, from L.A. to Chicago—and you're number one."

Me? The top salesperson out of ten thousand?!

For my innovation, I was number one in the company. Number one in the nation. In the country.

I had the thought that I was brilliant. Maybe for the first time in my life. I was walking on air.

But it didn't last long.

Because the voice on the phone kept talking, and I felt its tone dim. The voice proceeded to tell me, in some roundabout (sugarcoated) way, that because I hadn't "put in the work" they didn't think I deserved it.

I may have been brilliant, but I sure could be stupid. Because, for some reason, I replied, "Yeah, maybe you're right."

So they fired me, citing something about work ethic. Basically, they fired me because I had beaten the 'big boys' in the office. And the men weren't having it. I came up with an idea and executed it in an out-of-the-box way. I was crushing it, and the company was making tons of money of me. I feel it maybe embarrassed them a bit—like, how did a little old 24-year-old girl beat out all the long-tenured males in the office?

But they still fired me. They fired their number one sales rep in the country. Yep.

And to throw salt on this the wound, salt that really stung, they gave my *entire* business over to an older guy, married with children, because, in their mind, "he deserved it." That's what they told me. Some pot-bellied cowboy boot-wearing dude with no college degree and a complete zilch in the mojo category "deserved" the revenue stream I had created and built.

WTF hadn't quite been created yet, but I said a lot of versions of the sentiment.

I built the biggest flood of orders the company had ever seen, but I was not thanked with a Rolex watch or even a raise. I was fired.

At that moment, I knew I would never again build something for any other company but my own.

Looking back, it was a defining moment in my life. A true UnCaging experience.

After about eight months of schoolwork and time spent enjoying spending my newly earned money, I was sitting on my friend's couch on a Sunday afternoon. Her boyfriend was watching a football game, and after the third quarter he gets up to get a beer as the commercials start.

An infomercial comes on—the voice in my memory is like God's as he hands Moses the Ten Commandments: "Do you want to make money, for *yourself?*" it says. "Do you want to start your own business?"

I'm on the couch nodding like a kid looking at cotton candy. "Yes!" I say, my girlfriend giving me an odd look. "Yes!"

The voice on the screen goes on to talk about how their seminar teaches you how to buy and sell real estate notes. It wasn't really my field but who cares—all I heard was "*You build the business. You own the business. You make your own money.*"

I got the info for their free event. I attended, learned more, and bought the three-day paid seminar.

But the real skill was this: To get the seminar for $1,000 and not the regular cost of $3,000, I wrote down that I was someone's spouse. (Though the game can be fucked up, sometimes you have to use the rules to your advantage). But the great thing? They knew I had lied— and they *liked* it. They thought it showed tenacity. They thought it showed self-promotion savvy.

So I got my discount and went out to the seminar and attended for three days. It was super valuable information. And they like my tenacity so much that they hired me to work for them.

Two months after that football Sunday I moved to Florida to boldly embark down a new and exciting path; a path that led me to travel around the country with icons of the real estate world. I'm talking sales gurus and legends.

They became my mentors. I started just being a sponge around them, and that's when my education really began. My real-life education in business and entrepreneurship.

Because, while we are taught to 'go to school' and go in debt because the professors will teach us everything we need to know to get a great job and it'll be completely worth it. . . that's crap.

The real-life applications taught in America's colleges and universities are pretty much non-existent.

The art of making the type of money that gives you the freedom to do whatever you want is the art of *sales persuasion*. It's the art of the deal. And you just don't get that in college. You get that by being out there and doing it.

School can teach you a skill, a tactic, but it doesn't teach you the psychology of business that will transform that skill into value for the marketplace.

I didn't learn *anything* about making money in college, and I learned very little about it from corporate America. I learned about making money through mentors, through working with them, through traveling with them, through soaking up whatever I could from them.

They gave me the experience and the moves to move down the pipeline to where I needed to go.

They were so important. And good mentors are hard to find. When you find one, learn as much as you can as quickly as you can. Check your ego at the door because I'll tell you that along my journey, I've screwed up a bunch when I thought I knew shit when I didn't know shit.

Most real-world knowledge does not come from a university. It comes from the people you meet along the path who have been there before—who have paved the road upon which you can walk.

When you're lucky enough to find a mentor, soak up the knowledge like a thirsty sponge. If you do that as an entrepreneur, you will make a lot more money in a lot less time. Be coachable.

I once had this client who paid me half my fee upfront but when the job was done, she refused to pay the other half. And I'd already given her the product. Yeah, you're not supposed to do that, I know. But she said she'd pay me.

I emailed her to remind her of the invoice. No response. I texted. No response. My calls went straight to voicemail and her call-backs were late and infrequent. The energy became excruciating. It wasn't make-or-break money, but it was a fairly considerable amount.

I did a self-evaluation and after a time, the universe told me what to do.

I decided to forgive her for the rest of the invoice.

Why would I do that?

One, I believe in the universe, and what it is telling me. Two, the energy around the whole thing was excruciating; it wasn't serving either of us; it just seemed like with her mindset that she somehow *deserved* the money, the struggle to get the second half of my invoice was going to continue to be a struggle for a long time.

So the money I was owed became less important to me. Forgiving became the currency-energy of the moment.

It's an abundant world. If you see abundance, you will likely walk in an abundant world. With this in mind, I wrote the client a text that I would forgive the remainder of the invoice to release the energy surrounding it. I encouraged her to please donate the money to a non-profit of her choosing.

I pushed send and felt a good release.

Yet writing that text is not something I would have done a few years prior. It was a mentor of mine who taught this lesson to me.

Like my client, for a long time I held a view around money that I *deserved* it.

It took me a long time to understand that that's not how the universe works.

It's not "if you build it, they will come" or "if I build it, I deserve it." It's more like, "if I build it and create value to the marketplace and can sell it—over and over again—then it will *simply* come."

The mindset of "I deserve money" is the mindset of someone in big-corporate. It doesn't work with entrepreneurship. In entrepreneurship, you have to allow it.

Sure, part of me wanted to forgive that invoice as a "fuck you" (I may be UnCaged but I'm still no saint). But, after some meditation got me back to my grounded being, I knew that wouldn't work. If I were going to forgive the payment, I had to forgive it from a good space. So, I did.

And you know what? Just a couple days after releasing the energy from that payment, another client appeared. The work she wanted me to do for her was almost identical to what the previous client owed me.

That's the universe, babe.

UnCaged Lesson:

Be coachable. Learn from other entrepreneurs. Let it be and let it flow.

EASE OF ENTRY (FOR ELITE LEVEL PROFITS).

T he way I teach it (because I *know* it works) anyone who is in touch with their weird and in touch with their bold can start selling their products and make money online. If you have those two things, all you need next is get to know three little puzzle pieces.

These three pieces comprise what I call The Ultimate Influencer's Growth Triangle. They are the traingle's pillars—your media, your social audio, and your social media. It's simple and it works. The Ultimate Influencers Growth Triangle gets people to consume you, to buy from you, and to take action with you.

It starts with your media, or your media app, which is your podcast. Podcasting is the best and fastest way to get people to consume you, to eat you right up. With podcasting, you can push your voice, your content, around the world, fast. My students are currently broadcasting on over twenty-five networks around the globe.

The great thing about podcasts is where you upload your content. You are NOT uploading directly to YouTube or to Google or to Meta, but rather to your *own* server—a third-party hosting company. Once you do this, you use the RSS feed to push content to podcast networks around the world like Amazon Fire, Spotify, iHeart, Pandora, Roku, and a lot of others. The technology is not that hard to learn, and you can get your message out to a lot of people. You can create a buzz and find an audience.

I encourage you to do it.

Because when you place your voice on a third-party hosting company, you own the content and "they" can't take it down. You control the content. This gives you freedom of voice. You can talk about things that may be socially or politically taboo. You can cuss if that's your thing. You're kinda freed to just be able to be yourself.

This is why every television news anchor has their show *and* their podcast.

The podcast starts the conversation. If you are selling brownies without sugar, do a podcast on the benefits of a paleo diet. If you write books, tease out passages weekly. If you like to talk about relationships, do that.

Then, after you have your media, next comes the second pillar: getting your content repurposed. This gets you connected to a community that consumes your content. It essentially becomes 'the backstage pass' for your fans. It offers people who like what you are doing a more intimate platform, a place where they can come and learn more about you, get to know you.

The cost to repurpose your podcast audio content is nil. All it really costs is the time it takes to learn a few pieces of software.

In fact, none of this triangle-pyramid takes a lot of time or money. The hosting fee is flat-out cheap. The fact that a month's cost is pretty much equivalent to a fancy cocktail at a restaurant means *no excuses*. (And this chapter is the "E" chapter, so it just got subtitled, No Excuses!) Put your energy into this for three months, and it works. It does because I see it happen all the time.

Where was I? Right, no excuses, and… yes, the third pillar of the Ultimate Influencer Growth Triangle: Social Audio. This is where you create more content and, by doing so, form your relationships and community.

Whether it's Clubhouse, Wisdom, or whatever the social audio app of the moment comes to be named, the game is the same. And that game is getting people to consume as much of you as possible while they connect with you.

Sounds fun, right—the ability to engage and create a real-life community from just the power of your phone?

You don't even need video equipment. You don't need to get dressed. You don't need to do your hair or even brush your teeth if you don't want to. And it's LIVE.

The more people that can consume you on a social audio app, the more people have the opportunity to consume you and connect with you. Consumption time leads to trust—and trust leads to buyers.

Having you and your brand eaten up makes you a known leader. Hopefully a bold, weird, and badass leader and influencer. Because people buy from whom they feel connected to, because that releases them from confusion. When I work with clients in our mentorship program, the first thing we focus on is getting them to be clear on who they are—because when we become clear on who we truly are, we become clear on what we are truly selling. Which is a strong foundation.

Remember why? Because a confused mind never buys.

Once we are connected through the podcast and repurposed through our social audio, we move to conversion via social media. Conversion (purchases, income, money, freedom) happens through the DM's— through Direct Messages (via Meta, Instagram, Tik Tok, or SMS Messenger).

Here's why: regular social media is a *push*. You push a video; you push a post. Push, push, push, push, push. But money is not made in push marketing but through conversation marketing. You need to engage and ask and absorb and be. Not just push push. That's why your social media direct messages (DM's) are so important.

* * *

So, to sum up the Ultimate Influencer Growth Triangle: from your influence, we attract your audience. We do this through the podcast. From the podcast we move to the community, heightening our impact. Once we are consumed and engaged, utilizing our community, the conversion comes to fruition through the conversational aspects of social media.

That's why I teach that anyone in the world who has a phone can create a business from anywhere—any product, any service—to sell anytime.

In my courses, I show my clients how to do one podcast a week for fifty-two weeks and then turn them into 8,000-10,000 pieces of content to drip through social audio and social media throughout the year. We do this, of course, by repurposing content—our podcast becomes our talking points in the room, which become our conversation points on our page.

(Note: Meta, Instagram and Tik Tok are enough social media to make a brand. Also, if you really want a website, you can save a lot of time and money by using a microsite like Socialtap.com).

And while it is true that you don't get consumption without influence, that doesn't mean your podcast should take ninety percent of your energy. The connection and conversion through social audio and social media are equally, if not more important, than the content itself.

Business parable time:

About fifteen years ago my uncle got the bug to be a cool-guy fisherman. As a man with more behind him than in front of him, he had a vision and needed to see it through to actuality.

So, he went down to the Gulf of Mexico where he hired a guy to take him out for some bigtime fishing. He took me along as well. We drove down there and showed up at the harbor. The fisherman-dude guy looked the part and talked the talk. He was already making my uncle feel cool.

Then he took us out and into the Gulf. Like for a long time. Like for an hour and a half of boom-boom-boom over the wind-chopped water motoring out into the horizon.

I got seasick. I did. And my uncle, drinking his beer, did not. But I'm not here to talk about me or my uncle. I'm here to talk about the cool fisherman dude on the gulf, his brimmed hat pulled low and his tanned skin with steel-blue eyes. (And though he was h.o.t., I'm not here to talk about that either.)

I'm here to talk about how after he'd sped us out and out and out, he just stopped, in the middle of nowhere—nothing but teal waters and sky. He put down his radar tool and stopped the boat and cut the engine and said, coolly, "Here we go."

My uncle and I looked at him as he dropped a lure into the sea. Then another. Then another and another.

He put like 20 lures out—20 lures from one boat—because he had found where the fish were.

With one boat and many lures, the fisherman-dude guy had done his job. My uncle paid him a lot (a lot) of money for five hours of his time.

I say: Learn from the fisherman-dude guy. Your brand is your boat. And through your podcast, your social audio, and your social media, you can put out a whole lot of hooks in the water from essentially one boat.

Not just one hook but a bunch of hooks—into waters teaming with potential clients. That's the way to do it.

UnCaged Lesson:

UnCage Your Voice. Launch Your Voice.

Do It.

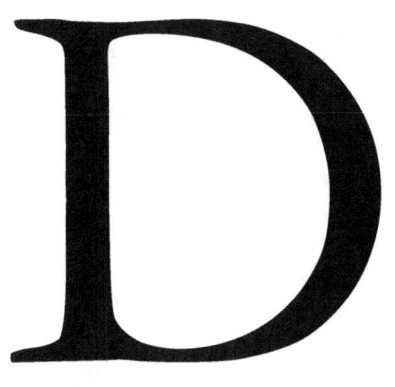

Dominate

TAKE A HIKE!!—TESTS ON THE TRAIL OF LIFE

I went on a date once that lasted four and a half minutes.

I met this guy on Bumble. He was a good-looking guy, late 50s, and he was the CEO of something or other and lived really close to me. In my head I was like, maybe he'll become a good business connection, some great new friend. *Who knows, right?*

I agreed to meet him, and he suggested we meet at the trailhead, Austin's Town Lake trail right there in the middle of the city.

That's a great first date," I thought. "Not dinner or a bar, what could go wrong? What could possibly go wrong on the hiking trail?"

Turns out, a lot.

Here's what went down. First, he was late. He texted me about being stuck in a meeting and I was thinking: it's the entrepreneur world, it's all good, I know how it goes. Worst case, I'll get some exercise out of this thing.

Finally, he showed up and got out of his car. He's attractive, he's in shape, and he's got a cute dog. I was looking super cute in my hat and my little shorts, and I figured, life is short, so we said "hi" and started out on our walk along the trail.

If you've ever been to Austin and walked the Austin Trail, you'd know it's pretty damn wide—three-or-four-people-and-a-couple-of-dogs-across type-wide. Even during the pandemic, people went there all the time to hold wonderfully amazing conversations six feet apart and still manage to walk side by side.

But as we started out on the trail, this guy immediately walked out ahead of me. Not side by side, but out front, walking directly in my path, way up ahead with his dog.

To me this was super weird, especially because he was talking like he was right by me, just looking straight ahead and asking questions to the air in front of him—making no attempt to even turn his head around or even sideways to see if I was following or if I could even hear what the heck he was saying.

"So, where ye from?" I managed to hear him say, and real intriguing questions like, "how long have ye been on Bumble?"

I was unengaged, but worse it was so weird. Why was he walking up in front of me and not to my right or left? I could barely hear him, let alone look at his face while he was talking. I was literally leap-stepping to keep up with him.

"Hey," I said finally, "would you mind pulling back so I can get up equal to you and we can talk?"

He muttered something about wanting the dog to be able to stretch his legs.

Alright fine, I thought (the dog *was* cute, Murphy was his name. Can't remember the guy's). But then the guy just kept speeding up, barging on ahead of me like it was windy and he was a kite.

I would strain to catch up, and then he would just go faster.

We were now at about the two-minute mark of the date.

For another ninety seconds or so he was striding along the trail in gigantic bounds with me chasing behind, pumping my legs as fast as I could without picking them up into a full-on striding jog.

"What the hell kind of "trail date" is this?" I thought. "If I knew we were going running, I'd have brought different shoes!"

There was nothing like what you might call 'conversation,' but I did manage to hear a few more of his questions as he again faced straight ahead and continued to walk on out front. I answered what I could hear and made up the rest.

We were four minutes into the date and it was excruciating. I couldn't take trying to keep up with this guy anymore. If he wouldn't walk beside me, I'd had it. So I started testing him. Because tests can be good. Just like clients will test you. Just like business partners will test you. I started pulling back, slowing down, seeing what he'd do. I wanted to see if he'd walk on or turn around and maybe even look me in the eye so we could walk together down the path.

He didn't. But I saw in his shoulders that he noticed something, that he finally noticed I wasn't right behind him anymore. He slowed down, a little, only enough to get back within earshot but remain far ahead.

Not, mind you, side by side.

I hollered out some question to him, He answered something I couldn't hear as he just walked on, talking to the wind in front of him.

"Hey," I hollered out again, "do you mind slowing down a little, coming back so we can be equal? I feel very subservient to you."

That one set him off. He swung around, his arms literally flying into the air. "Ahhh!" he yelled. "You crazy woman!"

4:27, 4:28, 4:29.

This date was over.

There were no more words needed.

If another human being isn't going to walk side by side with you, isn't going to give a little eye contact every once in a while, don't waste your time. Whether on a date or a business call, if you see this, move on.

So I laughed to myself and turned around and jogged back to my car. At least I got some exercise.

Still, in this, the shortest date of my life (never to be broken, so help me God!) I learned something. Rather, I was *reminded* of something. Something important, and it is this:

Dating is like marketing, and sales is like sex.

Tests will be given. Conversation is key. You have to know, to like, to trust, to understand both what you can provide and what you need.

Just like that terrible date with the unforgettable Bumble Dude on the Austin Trail, when a potential client freaks out at the littlest thing, peace out. It's a test and they didn't pass; just like how women test men and how men test women, entrepreneurs must test their clients.

You will be giving this person your time and it better be worth it.

Good clients will test you too.

That's when it gets fun.

The tests are what help us grow, what help us become better.

Clients and business partners will test you and sometimes even piss you off. But "the test" is worthy in and of itself. It shows that your client/partner has a little edge to them. A little passion, a little fight. The ideal client or work-partner is not the quiet person who perpetually nods their head and never ruffles any feathers. That's boring. And it doesn't create *anything*. Nothing good anyway.

We're all different. We all have our truths. Strong-willed people can and will see things differently. Opinions will be voiced. This is good, and this must never stop in your career as an UnCaged Entrepreneur because the great thing about 'tests' is that they help us see what we did not see before.

Because, with that initial battle, those pointed words and the heated debate, commonalities do and will emerge. Commonalities that, due to a little discussion, have come to light—oftentimes in new and exciting combinations and trajectories.

To get to the buried treasures laying hidden on the bottom of the ocean floor, you have to ruffle up some sand. People are the same way. Real jewels can and do exist just below the surface. Often it just takes a good test to help them shine.

When they do, true connections are made. And once we get on this level with another human being, we can truly start to do dynamic business with them.

So, the lesson of the day? It's not how you enter the room but how you exit that people remember. Let people see how you *respond* more than how you *react*. Give people the opportunity for you to show up as a leader.

UnCaged Lesson:

Let people test you.

CHALLENGES & LEGACY

I once read an article where Lebron James talks about how before games he'll scroll the internet and social media for haters, looking for people talking shit about him so he can use that angry energy toward on-court greatness. Though Lebron reigned as the best basketball player on the planet for a long darn time, he continually sought motivation to keep him sharp. Kind of like the Depression-era racehorse Seabiscuit in the movie (or in real life) making eye contact with the competing horse to fuel his stride. A challenge, a little chip on the shoulder, can be a very motivating thing. Anger can be a motivating energy force.

Lebron James knew that if he started to take in all the praise of him being 'The King,' if he took the bait and began to believe that he was truly at the mountaintop, there would have been nowhere higher for him to go.

That's why Lebron was always looking for what's next.

So am I.

You should be too.

Part of my mission is to help one million women start and run their own businesses. I know, pretty high-scope goal.

I told someone about this mission early in 2020. Have you ever heard of 'The Undercover Billionaire' Grant Cardone? Well, you should have. He's pretty big-time. And so is his wife, Elaine Cardone, author of *Build Your Empire*.

I caught the ear of her assistant and was on the phone with her: "Yeah, I'm on a mission to help ten thousand women," I told her, proudly.

There was a brief pause on the line. "Is that *it?*" she asked.

I was a little taken aback.

"You should make it a million," she said. "If you want to talk with Elaine and Grant, you should add some more zeros."

"Think bigger?" I asked.

"Think bigger."

We talked a bit more and then said goodbye. *Not many people ever challenge me like that,* I thought. Not many people throw down the gauntlet like that.

But I've always liked a good challenge.

And because of that conversation, I started thinking bigger. Started thinking of how to bring Female Financial Sovereignty to the globe. Not just to ten thousand women but a friggin' million. Maybe I'll make it there, maybe I won't. But I will try. And now I know I'll help much more than ten thousand women.

Why?

Because of a challenge.

Which builds off another, older challenge.

Let's get down to it.

I've had some bad luck with men.

I was abused by my father.

I was abused by more than a couple of boyfriends.

And, after I'd just made my fiancé $1.5 million, one day he took out a gun, put it firmly against my head, and threatened to kill me. Then he ripped off my clothes, threw me against a wall, and attempted to rape me.

That was a bad moment. Needless to say, that moment has changed me, but it does not define me.

And although I know it is not my fault, one main reason that situation happened was that I let that fiancé of mine handle the finances. *My* finances. Because of old programming that "men are better at money than woman."

That was a Cage of mine.

The moment he placed that gun to my head, I can still see it in my mind's eye, I saw the Cage. The Cage that I had placed myself inside. The Cage that my mother, my grandmother, and my great-grandmother had all been in. That is when I started my mission to help women launch their own businesses so they could have real financial sovereignty.

But first, I had to create mine.

So I left that guy. No more. With nothing to my name, no money, no business, I drove down the road to the jewelry store and hawked my engagement ring for a couple grand.

And I started over. Again.

I never want to see another woman in that situation, dependent solely on a man and without options. I pray no one ever gets into a situation like I did, but even if it's not violent—even if the cage is just a feeling or a perception—I want people to be able to get out. To be able to be independent. To have the freedom to choose.

Helping female entrepreneurs is my legacy play. I want to be remembered as a financially sovereign female, a badass businesswoman who left her mark to help one million women become financially sovereign. That is why I created my mentorship program. That is why I am doing the things that I am doing.

I have chosen my path. In doing so, I broke open at least one cage.

I feel kind of like one of those cape-wearing superheroes in the movies, maybe even like the Greek hero, Achilles. You may remember that the universe put a metaphoric gun to his head too.

After the Trojan prince Paris stole Helen from the Greeks to start the Trojan War, Achilles was informed by the gods that he had two choices:

He could remain at his home and live a long, happy life with his wife and raise many children—but after they were gone, his name would be forgotten.

Or, he could choose to go fight at Troy. If he went to battle, he would live a short life—but his heroic deeds would be remembered for all of time.

If we've ever read Homer's *Iliad* or seen Brad Pitt in *Troy*, we know Achilles chose 'the legacy play.'

Julius Caesar, Catherine the Great, Steve Jobs, Lebron James, Martha Stewart. At one point in their lives, they all realized they had enough power, enough innovation, and enough money to simply stop and chill. But they kept going. To cement their legacy. To find out truly how far they could go.

One of the things that helped me find out how far I could go was meeting Martha. I met her in New York City in November of 2019 at Carnegie Hall.

It changed my life forever.

See, Martha Stewart is a funny woman. Hilarious actually. But she's got this cold-streak essence to her, like a focused animal or something. She is clear on who she is and where she is going. I could feel it and see it in her.

Before we all knew her, Martha was this rich housewife in the Hamptons back before she was famous. She had enough money to never do anything but bake and host parties. But she wanted more. She wanted to be more tomorrow than she was yesterday. So, she wrote a book, her first book, about wedding cakes.

It was a huge success. She could have stopped there, rested on her laurels as a bestselling author and enjoyed watching the waves curling up the shore for the rest of her life. Obviously, she didn't. She created an empire. Because she wanted to. Because she chose to.

But then she got busted for insider trading (whatever, she was beating the big boys and they got pissed. Sound familiar?) She was shamed by society. She went to jail. For twelve months. An entire year.

When I met her, she'd been out for a bit and she told me that she called jail, "Yale." Like "yeah, I hung out at Yale for twelve months and wore orange." And she said it in this very I-don't-give-a-fuck way.

I loved it. Martha owned it, didn't back down from her reality. And she used the time wisely. She talked with her other inmates, other women she was serving with. Many of them were middle-class women, you know, her target market, her buyers. And so, she asked them questions, learned what they wanted. She used her time as great Direct-Response Research.

When Martha got out she took a day to get her hair done, get her nails done, and get a facial. Then she was right back out on the warpath.

The next day, she said f*ck the networks and f#ck the big advertisers and she called little old PBS. And Martha got back on-air, on Martha's terms.

Without the large budget she was used to, Martha knew she'd have to hire her own director, her own producer, her own editor, and so forth. She'd have to hire her own crew. So she forked the bill and did it. She needed to get back on the horse and cement her legacy. She doubled down her workload and started filming not one show a week, but three.

Martha Stewart had UnCaged from the clink and was ready to UnCage from the haters.

She did what she needed to do. That chip on her shoulder had gotten pretty heavy, and Martha the stone-cold baker-bitch rebuilt her empire. In a big damn way.

So, UnCager, I'm just gonna ask: What are you going to "go for" that will leave a lasting legacy?

UnCaged Lesson:

Burn the past. Envision the future. Create your legacy.

D IS FOR DOMINATE.

The D of the UnCaged method stands for Dominate—Dominate, Disrupt, and Do good. These are the culminating steps that take you from "having a few good ideas" to cashing in on them so you can live that badass life of ultimate freedom.

And those 'Ds' start with investing in yourself. Dominate by investing in your leadership and your growth—dominate in your personal growth and development. Finally and truly become an influencer and creator.

And once you get super clear on your message and your audience, then you DOMINATE your competition.

We do this by making our message to our audience omnipresent. In the online world, you can be everywhere, all the time, all at once. Do it. Dominate your niche.

Dominating is a mindset, a mindset that we can always create more content, be better, be everywhere, and be more efficient with our time.

It's about constantly leveling up and dominating the landscape. And the first landscape you must learn to dominate is your own mind. Because you can't let it dominate you.

This is the essence of this book and the essence of my coaching program: To make an impact and grow that seven-figure (or higher) business, you have to disrupt your old mindset patterns and do something new and bold and UnCagy.

You are not what you were when you were a kid. Your past does not define your future.

Not unless you let it.

You will come into influence, impact, and income when you break free from what is expected of you.

Your goal as an entrepreneur should be nothing less than to impact the world. To make *the world* a better place.

Your voice matters. Your message matters.

And one voice can change the world.

This reminds me of a YouTube video I just watched. It showed the story of a woman who changed Barack Obama's world back when he was running for president; the video was of her voice, in the back of a small room, in a small townhall meeting. "Fired-Up!" she chanted loud. "Ready. To. Go!"

Then another voice chimed in. "Fired Up! Ready. To. Go!"

Another joined in, and another—until Barack even started shouting it out himself.

Soon the whole room was on their feet and crying out, "Fired Up! Ready. To. Go!"

All because of one voice. One voice from the back of the room. That one voice got the vibrations going.

You may think that your message, your voice and your service do not matter.

This is incorrect.

Because I am here to remind you in a whisper of something that you already know…

Your Time is now. You are ready.

Please, feel the power of the spoken word and read this next sentence out loud:

I am ready.

Read it again.

I am ready!

Scream it out loud!

My Time is Now! I am ready!!

Yes, you are. Your time is now.

◆•▬—•—▬●▬—•—▬•◆

Entrepreneurship is a spiritual practice. To illustrate this, I'm going to close by talking about a spiritual guy. A spiritual business guy. Christian or not, a fan of him or not, you've probably heard of him: Joel Olsteen.

What always gets me about preachers is that every single one of them is working from the same material. They all teach from the same book. The Big Book. The Bible. They preach from the same proverbs and teach the same lessons.

In a two-thousand-year-old how-to manual, nothing should be revolutionary, right?

Well, Olsteen *is* a revolutionary. For, every year of my adult life, his church has been either first or second in endowments. Some churches can't keep the lights on yet Joel's is kicking ass and taking names (in a Christian way). Last I checked, his Lakewood Church was averaging $230 million a year in donations, income, and endowments.

In short, Joel is dominating. Has been dominating. Will continue to dominate, because he understands the value of influence and distribution. He understands that he is paid for his value in the marketplace.

And he understands media—the power of media distribution.

While Joel loves the parables and the stories and the book from which he teaches, he knows that his reach is not just based upon the stories he tells. Anyone can pick up a bible (or stay at a motel and reach in the drawer) and read what he is reading.

So, what is making the difference here? All pastors have the same 'content,' and content is supposed to be king, right?

Well, Joel's genius lay in his background in radio, and how he adapted what he learned to grow his church.

A lot of people think he inherited the mega-church upon which he now reigns. Wrong. While his father did leave the church to him, Joel took it from fledgling to fantastic because of his understanding of media—and his desire to dominate in distribution.

He surrounded himself with people like Tony Robbins and took the time to develop relationships with other pastors. He knew the game of personal brand marketing and influence branding. He understood how to create reach-authority distribution. And then, he did something genius. He got on Sirius XM—where he is on-air twenty-four hours a day, three-hundred and sixty-five days a year.

He dialed his sermons down to a science—a spiritual science. He preaches once a week for twenty-two minutes. Exactly twenty-two minutes—the exact amount of time he has for his half-hour time slot. He records once a week for twenty-two minutes and then banks the recordings, dripping them out whenever he wants.

How? Because he keeps his content as evergreen as evergreen can be. He never mentions dates or times of year. If he's recording on December 23, he never talks about the "upcoming Christmas holiday." Not a mention of Valentine's Day or Easter or Boxing Day.

Because he wants his sermons, which play on that twenty-four-seven, three-six-five, round-the-clock schedule, to be readily absorbed no matter when his audience listens to them.

Even during the pandemic, he never mentioned the word Covid. Not one mention of Corona, testing centers, or getting the vax. Nope, he said things like "we are going through challenging times" and "circumstances can be difficult." He spoke about "trying ordeals" and elucidated the parables that help him get through such ordeals.

That's because Joel Olsteen is strategic as hell (or heaven, I suppose). He understands the principles I teach. He understands the principles of influence. And he does his work to "Do Good." He believes one hundred and twenty percent in what he does—and he knows that to dominate distribution and his target market with the tools available to him, he will:

1.) attain the most influence,

2.) sow the greatest impact, and

3.) reap the most income for his church so he can give back to his community.

1) Joel has succeeded in having his message heard and in keeping the lights on for his congregation. He's succeeded in becoming omnipresent. He's succeeded in dominating.

Let's circle back. Back to content. It may be King, but the distribution of the content is Queen. And Queens are the most powerful pieces on the chessboard.

With that, here are the steps that successful entrepreneurs and creators use to create influence, income, and impact. I call them G.R.O.W.

Here are the steps to grow your audience, build your list, and scale your sales.

- **G**et clear on who you serve and what their biggest challenge is that you can help solve.
- **R**efine your brand to your ready-to-pay audience and create 'demand for your brand.'
- **O**btain massive audience share by dominating your lead-gen to become omnipresent in your distribution.
- **W**in sales and scaling by leveraging your message to reach more buyers than ever before.

It's time to G.R.O.W.

I see it in my yearlong mentorship programs all the time, with the female entrepreneurs I work with. I see them focused on building a successful business without sacrificing. I see my clients creating what they've always wanted to. I see people interested in business becoming entrepreneurs. I see people UnCaging. I see my clients putting fear behind them so they can do what they are called to do. I see scalable businesses that have the impact, influence, and healthy income that everyone deserves.

I see this stuff happen with my clients all the time. And I know that you can do it too.

If you want it, you can do it.

ONWARD

I'll end this little book where I started it: with a story. Because every good ending has a new beginning in there somewhere.

This final story is the story of a client of mine, the story of a person out there in the world who wanted to do more with her life. Her name is Jacquia.

Jacquia is a woman in her 30s looking to do something new with her life. She heard about one of my weekend-long podcasting intensives and signed up. She wanted to learn something dynamic, so she made the time and committed to the workshop.

I was excited to work with her.

The weekend came, but for the entirety of Saturday's virtual group course, her video screen was blacked out! I couldn't see her. And she wasn't speaking much either. She was so quiet that I came to wonder what the heck she was doing on her end; if she was even there at all.

After the session was through and everyone had said our goodbyes, I wasn't sure if I was going to see Jacquia again for day two. I wasn't sure if I would get to see Jacquia again, ever.

Oh, but I saw her.

At 5 a.m. on Sunday I'm up and doing my morning routine, preparing to teach my course—when my phone buzzes. I walk over to the table and pick it up. I open up the new audio text and push play—and I hear her. I hear Jacquia.

I hear this UnCaging woman half-singing, half-crying, half-laughing. Actually, let me rephrase that: *full*-singing, *full*-crying, *full*-laughing into the phone, singing to me at five o'clock in the morning with the words,
     "I am the voice, I am the voice, I am the voice..."

And then, still in song, I hear and see her: "Heather," she says, "you are the first person who has moved me to believe in my own voice…"

I was in tears.

The audio went on.

Jacquia kept speaking.

She shared. She gave. She opened up about her past so she could move forward into her future.

She told me how she had been in the armed forces, that she was a veteran, and that she had been injured in the field.

She also told me how when she was serving, she had been raped. By a superior. And how she had not been believed when she brought it to light. And how for getting raped in the military she ended up getting dishonorably discharged.

Jacquia told me her story, the story of being wounded by the enemy and raped by her own team, how she had been kicked out of her livelihood without benefits or a plan.

Yep.

And after a day of my podcasting weekend and a night to absorb and process the message of UnCaging, Jacquia was singing to me about how she felt—how for the first time in a long time she felt that she *mattered*, that she was *heard*. That she had a voice. And that she now believed in that voice.

Today? Well Jacquia broke down her cage in a big way. She started up her own podcast, and she's doing awesome. She's being heard. She's helping people, especially women and young girls of color. That was the path within her. And she's begun to walk it, boldly.

Jacquia has been spreading her influence to make the type of impact that earns her the income to spread more influence. Jacquia did what she needed to do.

She UnCaged.

And through that 5 a.m. message—in her own awesomely weird and unique way—Jacquia told me that I was playing a huge part in her UnCaging, that what I said and how I said it had made an instant impact on her life.

These are the moments I live for. These are the moments I wrote this book for. These are the moments I UnCage for.

Yes, I teach marketing. Yes, I teach business marketing. Yes, I teach people how to expand their influence, how to build their audience, how to make an impact with others, how to receive more income and more impact by helping more people than they ever thought imaginable.

But why I really do what I do is to nudge people into the belief that they matter—to help people feel, to know, that you have a voice.

Because I get what it is like to be told to fit into a box. I get what it is like to be told to "shut up and look pretty." (Or just to "shut up.")

We all, in our own way, have been told to 'shut up,' that we are 'too much.'

Use it.

UnCage with it.

That's one of my favorite things about my consulting/coaching work. I get to help people double down on the things within us that are not normal. Because that's what helps us get heard. That's what helps us get influence.

I'm living my mission. And it is the Jacquias of the world that inspire me and keep my flame going.

What I do is really quite simple, and you can do it too. I help people understand that they matter, that what they have to say matters, and that their knowledge is valuable—to the market and to the world.

And so here at the end of this little book I hope you know that YOU matter, now, more than you know.

Because when you UnCage yourself you UnCage your influence. And UnCaging your influence UnCages your voice. Which UnCages your story. Which UnCages your confidence. Which UnCages you to help others.

Which UnCages your prosperity.

And that's when you start singing in the shower at five in the morning— because you know you're about to turn your dreams and your desires into reality.

Marketing and scaling your creations is not really that hard. If I can do it, you can do it. However, it is harder if you are not in the right environment, if you are not learning through the best mentor, if you are not a part of a great supportive community.

UnCaging is about commitment over convenience; determination over fear; believing over doubting; vulnerability over being closed off.

Vulnerability? I suppose I will close with that.

See, for years I kept all of my failures, all my heartaches, and all my mistakes bottled up inside. In silence. Even just a couple of years ago, there was no way I would have shared a lot of the stories I shared in this book; I would have been worried about what you thought of me.

Not anymore.

I have arrived at a place of being open to being vulnerable. I am open to sharing my personal and private failures and successes—because they are an integral part of who I am today.

Our strength lay in our vulnerability. Ask Brene Brown. She says it this way:

"Stay Brave. Try to be aware of your armor. When you feel vulnerable, try to stay human, keep leaning."

Become vulnerable with your story and allow yourself to become a dynamic self-promoter of YOU.

Give yourself permission to UnCage. Give yourself permission to be weird. Give yourself permission to tell your story so you can make a boatload of money.

The only permission you need is your own.

And most importantly, Uncager: always know and believe that you are important, that you can and will do great things if you let yourself.

Break free from your cages to finally and ultimately be yourself. You are ready. Your voice is ready. Your time is now.

Be You. Be REAL. Be the boss of your life!

xoxo,

Heather Ann Havenwood

ACKNOWLEDGEMENTS

I want to thank all of the amazing people who helped me in the long journey of this book. It started out as a Pandemic Project in early 2020 and ended up being a journey all by itself.

Thank you to Jonathan Grant for all of your writing and editing and most importantly for your encouragement and faith in me along the way. I Appreciate you. You are a Gift and truly UnCaged!

I want to give a special thank you to Stephanie Pierucci— thank you for being an inspiration and for empowering me to UnCage my voice.

I also thank all of you, my readers. Be you. Be REAL. Be the boss of your life.

www.ingramcontent.com/pod-product-compliance
Lightning Source LLC
Chambersburg PA
CBHW060537130626
46553CB00002B/787